The Vanishe

The Vanished Path

BHARATH MURTHY

HarperCollins *Publishers*

HarperCollins *Publishers*

P-ISBN: 978-93-5177-019-0
E-ISBN: 978-93-5136-020-6

2 4 6 8 10 9 7 5 3 1

HarperCollins *Publishers*
A-75, Sector 57, Noida, Uttar Pradesh – 201301, India
1 London Bridge Street, London, SE1 9GF, United Kingdom
Hazelton Lanes, 55 Avenue Road, Suite 2900, Toronto, Ontario M5R 3L2
and 1995 Markham Road, Scarborough, Ontario M1B 5M8, Canada
25 Ryde Road, Pymble, Sydney, NSW 2073, Australia
195 Broadway, New York, NY 10007, USA

Typeset in 12/12 Actionist

Printed and bound at

Contents

Then a certain monk went to the Blessed One
and, on arrival, having bowed down to him,
sat to one side. As he was sitting there,
he said to the Blessed One:
'The world, the world', it is said.
In what respect does the word 'world' apply?
Insofar as it disintegrates, monk, it is called 'the world'.

From the Samyutta Nikaya, Sutta Pitaka, first century BCE.

1.
Wheel of Dhamma

PPAAAAAA
TAGA TAGA TAGA
Hello, Uncle, we were thinking of changing our plan—
No need, I found out that there is no curfew tomorrow in Varanasi, so you can proceed as scheduled—
Okay, bye.
The Ayodhya dispute verdict is tomorrow! Let's hope there's no violence. I think we should stick to plan and get off at Varanasi.
Ya ... if we go to Patna instead, it will upset our schedule, no?
TAGA TAGA
22451

You wanted to extend up to Patna, right?

Uh ... No, we will get off at Varanasi.

As long as you are on the train, I am at your service, but outside, you're on your own.

Your ticket ...

DIP

Alka, look outside, floods in UP!
RUPA

Hello! Haan!
Verdict is postponed?
Okay, okay...

Train number 12392,
New Delhi-Rajgir
Shramjeevi Express,
has arrived on
platform number two
HOWRAH

वाराणसी
VARANASI
Don't take the auto, I'll get you a rickshaw.
Uh ...

Ey rickshaw, take them to a decent hotel, okay?
...

That man told me he shifted here from Delhi ... has a garment business.
WHOO...
WHOW
WHOW
Srr...Srr...

The next morning.
ना रैश
ना खुजली
SUTHOL
TRRR...
STOP
We need to ask where the ASI guest house is.
Tatarr
Pattarr
We had managed to secure accommodation in the quaint old guest house of the Archaeological Survey of India at Sarnath.

Sarnath, known as Isipatana back then, is the place where Siddhatta Gotama, the Buddha, gave his first discourse to five sramana companions after his Awakening at the age of thirty-five (450—440 BCE), thus setting in motion the Wheel of Dhamma.

Siddhatta Gotama lived around 480—400 BCE. He died at the age of eighty after teaching for forty-five years. This teaching is called the Dhamma (Dharma in Sanskrit), which is how Buddhism has been known since it began. While teaching, he often referred to himself as the Tathagata, 'The One Thus Gone'.

Having spread across Asia over 1,500 years, Buddhism was forgotten for nearly 800 years in the land of its origin, its monuments abandoned to ruin. Sir Alexander Cunningham, founder of the Archaeological Survey of India in 1861, initiated a series of excavations that led to the rediscovery and restoration of these historical sites.

Stupa at Sarnath before restoration.

At the spot of the Tathagata's first discourse — called Dhammacakkappavattana Sutta, or Turning of the Wheel of Dhamma — Ashoka, the Buddhist emperor, built one of many brick stupas. This one is now popularly called Dhamek stupa. Over the centuries, it was built over, and by the fifth century CE, the Gupta kings had it extended and covered with beautiful patterned stone.
Ascending the Mauryan throne in 269 BCE, about 150 years after the Tathagata's death, Ashoka was the first monarch to actively promote the new faith in his domains and beyond.
PREE PREE

PREE
PREE

In 1794, the year Sarnath was rediscovered as a Buddhist site, Jagat Singh, Dewan of the Raja of Banaras (then under the control of the British East India Company), had ordered that the still standing Dhammarajika stupa, built by Ashoka, be dismantled and the bricks be used for new buildings.
While digging, they came upon a green marble casket inside a stone box. It held bone relics, some ornaments and gems. Jonathan Duncan, the British resident in Banaras, was alerted, and he wrote an account of it. The casket is now lost, but the stone box is in the Indian Museum, Kolkata.
Jonathan Duncan became governor of Bombay Presidency the very next year, and there is a curious memorial to him at the St. Thomas Cathedral, Mumbai, to this day. The memorial's central image is a large casket.

This is all that
remains of Ashoka's
30-metre-high
Dhammarajika stupa.

Look at all these miniature stupas!

These are votive stupas; devotional offerings, gifted by pilgrims, often inscribed with a dedication. Some are also memorials and could contain a relic inside.

A common dedication in Pali on these stone-and-clay offerings reads:

Ye dhamma hetuppabhava
tesam hetum tathagato aha,
tesanca yo nirodho
evam vadi mahasamanno.

Of those phenomena that arise from a cause,
the Tathagata has said, this is their cause,
and this is their cessation.
Thus the Great *Samana teaches.

Uff! So hot!

MINERAL

*Samana/Shramana. Homeless wandering ascetic who rejects brahminical scripture. Many Indian religious and philosophical traditions grew from this, including Buddhist and Jain.

clic
clic
clic
clic

))))))))))) 00))))
00)))) 0)))) 0)...
Indian guides speaking fluent Italian!

This is a rare example of a monolithic stone railing from the Mauryan period of the third century BCE.
Such a railing once crowned Ashoka's Dhammarajika stupa.

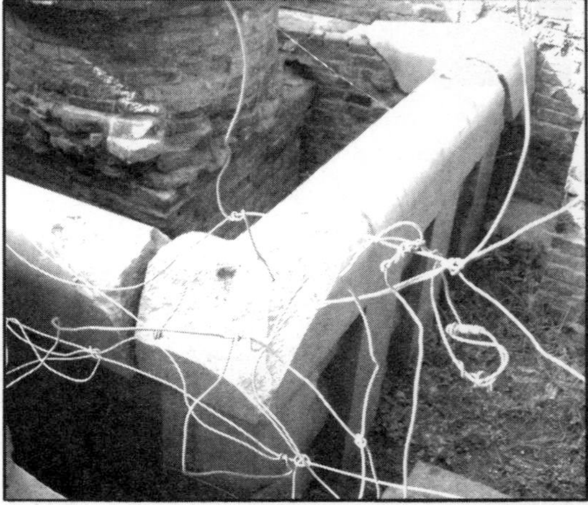

Ah! There's the Ashoka pillar.
In the Brahmi inscription, Ashoka warns against discord in the Sangha.
Hallo ... feeding deer ...
Hallo ... come ... feeding deer ...
Let's get some of that papaya. How much?

Ten rupees.
The Lion capital of the Ashoka pillar, which the Indian Constitution adopted as the official state emblem at the behest of B.R.Ambedkar, was discovered only in 1905, during excavations carried out by F.O.Oertel.
Iconic Buddha image from 5th c.CE
Ashoka pillar

Do you know English?
Haan ... A B C D E F G H ...
... X Y Z.
Very good. Which class?
Second standard.
What is your name?
Kiran.
Are you Buddhist?
No, Hindu.

Ay ay ay ayayay...
ay ay ay ay

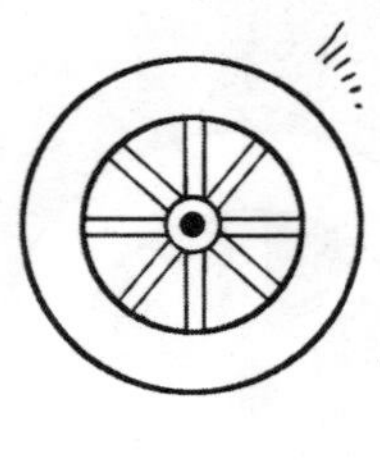

Bhikkus, this is the noble truth of suffering (dukkha): birth is suffering, old-age is suffering, sickness is suffering, death is suffering, being brought together with things disliked is suffering, separation from things liked is suffering, not to get what one wants is suffering.

Bhikkus, this is the noble truth of the cause of suffering: the craving for further existence that is associated with greed and satisfaction, that takes pleasure in this and that, namely, craving for the objects of the senses, craving for existence, craving for non-existence.

Bhikkus, this is the noble truth of the cessation of suffering: the complete cessation and fading away of that very craving; giving it up, letting go, being free, not tied to it.

Bhikkus, this is the noble truth of the practice leading to the cessation of suffering: just this Eightfold path, namely, right view, right intention, right speech, right action, right livelihood, right effort, right mindfulness, right concentration.

...
Welcome Alka and Bharath, please be seated. Listen and pay close attention. I will speak.
Bhikkus! As I was saying —
Uh, ex.... excuse me, sir.

Sorry to interrupt, but I was wondering why you have chosen to represent yourself as a wheel in this comic.

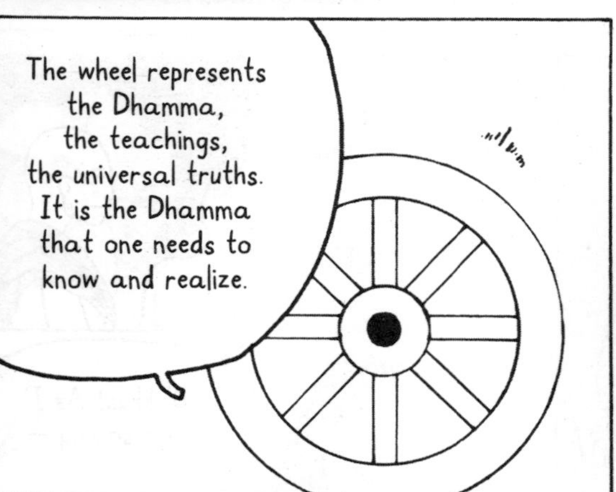

The wheel represents the Dhamma, the teachings, the universal truths. It is the Dhamma that one needs to know and realize.

In fact, during the early period of Buddhism, the Tathagata was represented mainly through symbols such as the Dhamma wheel, the bodhi tree, an empty throne, footprints.

The oldest preserved texts of the Tathagata's complete teachings survive in only one version, preserved in Pali, a literary language based on the various middle Indo-Aryan dialects spoken in the Ganga region during his time. Collectively known as the Tipitaka, or the three baskets — Sutta Pitaka, Vinaya Pitaka and Abhidhamma Pitaka — this version was written down in Sri Lanka in the first century BCE, about 350 years after the death of the Tathagata, and forms the canon of the Theravada tradition of Buddhism.

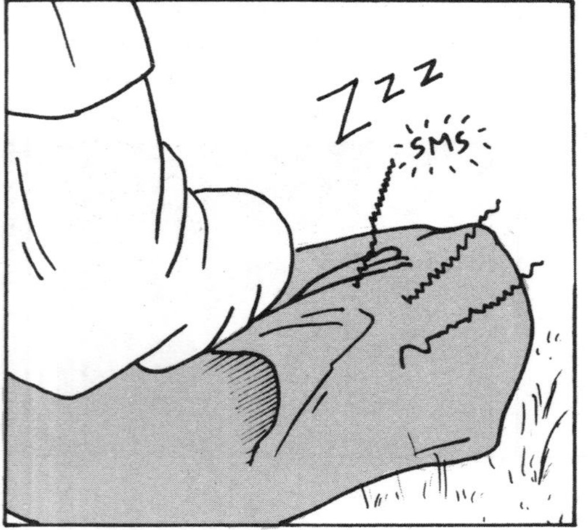
Z z z
SMS

Argh!
These spam SMSs!

Let's go eat something.

There seems to be only this one place here for food.
ARCHEOLOGICAL MUSEUM SARNATH
GREEN HUT
What do you get here?
Please check the menu.
*शिव आज भी गुरु हैं

Let's ask the ASI person about new excavations before going to Varanasi.
Ya, okay.
THUU!
Damn lock! Just won't close!
cloc cloc
KHAT
Uh, Srivastavji?
Yes, please go in.

Please sit. Tell me, what can I do for you?
A. SRIVASTAVA
Uh, we were interested in knowing if there have been any new excavations in this area.
Sir, one more sign, sir.
Scree
Scree
There have been no new excavations here since 1989.
Oh! Uh ... maybe if you could give us some information about Sarnath ... I am doing a comic about Buddhist sites in India.
My wife has written a book called Sarnath: Land of the Enlightened One. It has all the info, published in 2008.
Anything else?
Scree
Scree

Strange ... No excavations at all!

Will you go to Varanasi, to the ghats?
Sit.

TATARR
TRR

TAGA
TAGA
TAGA
TAGA

Autos are not allowed beyond this. You can take a rickshaw from here.

Pee!
Paa!
Rickshaw, madam?
Manikarnika ghat ...

BABA BLACK SHEEP
HOTEL AMMAN
गोदौलिया से विश्वनाथ मंदिर द्वार ← 700 मी०
PAPA PEEE

Dreading the ghats already! These rituals freak me out!
Me too. Somehow feels claustrophobic ...

You have to walk from here.
Bharath, wait ... I want to buy sunglasses.
Try this one. These plastic things are best I think.
Looks cool, no?
Hello. You want to buy goggles? This one is good, cheap.
How much?
250 rupees.
Let's take it.

Offering for Lord Shiva. Please take.
You also, please take!
He's smeared so much vermilion on my forehead. Good thing you told the police guy that you are allergic to vermilion and took just a pinch for yourself.
It's so difficult to refuse these guys! They just thrust themselves on you!
RUB
RUB

These cops are all over the place! Must be because of the Ayodhya verdict.
But remember there were bomb blasts here in 2006.

St. Peter English School
Play Group to V.
C.B.S.E.

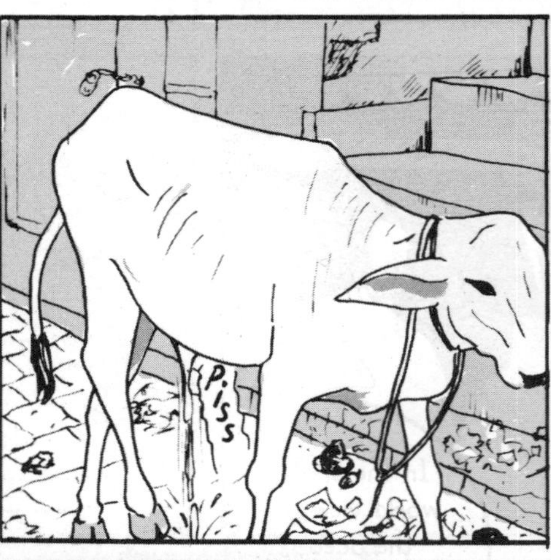
Piss

Chirr
When I look at Varanasi, I think about the end of Buddhism in India. When it disappeared from this land, Buddhism was a successful world religion — unlike brahminism, which had limited success in crossing over, in spite of its influence in South-east Asia.
In the brahminical world view, crossing the oceans was discouraged as leading to loss of caste identity.
Raam naam satya hai.
Raam naam satya hai.
Raam naam satya hai.

You know, when I came here to shoot that documentary, there wasn't so much water. It's totally flooded now!
Compared to Hindu Varanasi, Buddhist Sarnath seems like another world, even though it is only about 10 km from here.
...

Shankara wrote some of his commentaries on the Vedas here, right?

Ya, it's weird. He was here but he's not known to have visited Nalanda, which was the premier place of learning in his time.

Let's go ... it's claustrophobic here.

This gali is full of shit, and it's blocked.
BABA
DOLPHIN

A while later, we found ourselves back on the main road.

Let's start with the Chaukhandi stupa today.

We should also try and talk to some Buddhist monks if we can, no?
Ya, but we've hardly come across any yet.

clic !

This stupa, known as Chaukhandi stupa because of its four-armed plan, was constructed about 1,500 years ago, during the Gupta dynasty.
It marks the spot where the Tathagata met his five companion monks to whom he first taught the Dhamma.
The incongruous structure on top, built in 1588 CE, marks another historical moment, when Mughal emperor Humayun visited this area, long after Buddhism had vanished from here.

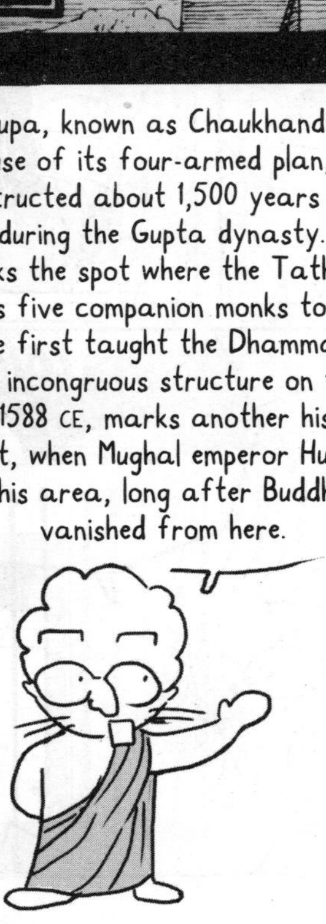

Such precise brick work, and so well preserved!
Huh? A makeshift Hindu temple right inside the archaeological site, blocking the exit.
TUN!
TUN!
Hallo! Which country? Ten rupees, open gate.
Huh? This is also business?
You speak Hindi?
Of course! We're Indian!

Do you live abroad?
No, we live in India only.

Are you married?
Yes.

Where is the bride from?
She is Bihari.

Ha! Ha! Alright! That's good.

Great, now open the gate please?

Ten rupees, open!

Why do they think we're foreigners?

Let's check out these new temples built for the pilgrim circuit.

FICE # DHARMAPALA MUSEUM # MAITRI BUDDHA TEMPAL
AHA BODHI SOCIETY OF INDIA
HE PIONEER INTERNATIONAL BUDDHIST ORGANISATION)

Anagarika Dharmapala, a wealthy Sinhalese whose father had become Christian, came under the influence of theosophists Madame Blavatsky and Colonel Olcott, who encouraged his conversion to Buddhism. He soon became influential in the formation of Sinhala Buddhist nationalism.

In 1891, he started the Mahabodhi Society. Its primary purpose was to wrest control of the Mahabodhi temple at Bodhgaya which was being run by Shaivite brahmin priests.

He died right here in Sarnath, in 1933, having been ordained a monk that same year. Though his moral character is not beyond reproach, enmeshed as he was in Sinhalese nationalist politics, his work was important in rekindling Buddhism in India.

You want guide, sir? I will not take money, sir.
I will show you Mulagandakuti Vihara, sir.
Sir, Thai tourists tying ribbon as offering to Lord Buddha.

Sir, this vihara build in 1931 by Anagarika Dharmapala, with donation of Mrs Mary Foster Wallace of Honolulu.

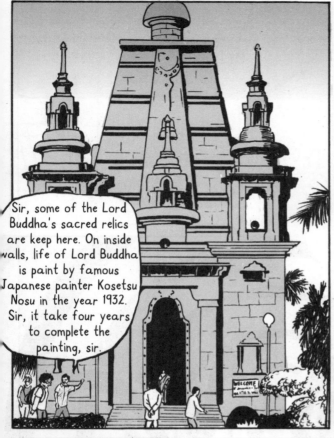

Sir, some of the Lord Buddha's sacred relics are keep here. On inside walls, life of Lord Buddha is paint by famous Japanese painter Kosetsu Nosu in the year 1932. Sir, it take four years to complete the painting, sir.

WELCOME

Sir, this is bodhi tree bring from Sri Lanka.

Sir, it is become night ... uh ... I explain you everything ... you can give whatever you like ... I show you Chinese monastery also ...

As we were leaving, at 6 p.m., the bell was rung at the vihara ...
DONG
... and the reverberation lasted for a long time afterwards.

2.
Birth is the Cause of Death

Hey Bharath, wake up, we're reaching Gorakhpur.

We need to find a hotel for tonight.

by Shahnawaz Fai

The next morning ...

... the Ayodhya verdict will be ...

You can take a jeep from the bus stand.

This town is named after a twelfth-century saint of the tantric Shaivite Nath sect.
Twelfth century? That's just when Buddhism ended out here.
Paa!
Pee!
Pooo...!

Sunouli! Sunouli!

You want to go to Sunouli?
No, Kushinagar.
Okay, come here.
You can pay for three seats, so you will be comfortable.
Okay, make some space here ...

SCREECH
Drrrr...
Three-and-a-half hours later.
Drrrr...

Let's go check the Chinese guest house and see if they have a place to stay.

You wait here, I'll go and inquire.

THESHUANG
BUDDHIST
KUSHINAGAR IND
ERECTED BY
REV KUOLEN BHIKSHU
HUNAN CHINE
WITH DONATIONS FRO
CHINESE OVERSEAS

That guy says they don't rent it to Indians, only foreigners! Ridiculous!
Indian guy?
Ya.

Just yesterday we were being mistaken for foreigners and now this! Let me go and talk.

At least give us a reason for not renting a room!
...

See, these local couples come and do bad things here, and the police come. Just yesterday, a few were caught.

Why don't you go to Pathik Niwas, it is run by the government.
LIN-SON
CHINESE BUDDHIST GUEST HOUSE
KUSHINAGAR
INDIA

So let's go to Pathik Niwas.
भाजपा

Kushinagar is little more than a village. All this Buddhist tourism seems recent.
WORLD TOURISM DAY
27 SEP. 201

LD TOURISM
DAY
27 SEP. 201

AAH... Achchoo

Hyuu ... I'm so tired from the jeep ride ... and I have a cold ...

Let's go to the cafe the travel guide recommends.

HOLY HIKING
POSTCARDS OF KUSHINAGAR AVAILABLE
TOUR ARRANGEMENT
YAMA CAFE
DELICIOUS FOOD
GIFT ITEM
FREE TRAVEL INFORMATION
Yama, god of death, at the death spot of the Buddha!

I need a hot lemon tea.
Sniff!

First, one hot lemon tea, and then one egg thukpa.
Hmmm. No chicken. Okay, I'll have one egg chowmein.

235 rupees.

Uh ... you people are doing some research ... some photography ... something?

I am actually writing a comic travelogue about Buddhist sites. It is also a pilgrimage — we are Buddhists.

Oh very good, very good! My name is T.K. Roy, and we run this cafe. Welcome to Kushinagar!

Are you Bengali?
Yes, yes, I'm Bengali. We have been here for many years.

We moved here in 1993. At that time, there were very few people here. Not developed, you know.

I was just wondering if you might have a guide or some information about Kushinagar.

Actually, I have written an article about it. I have a xerox copy.

Oh great! May I make a copy?
Yes, yes of course!
A Pillar of

Since you are doing some research and all that, you must meet Nandratna Bhikku. He is a very important person here. Come, come, I'll introduce ...

My wife ... and Nandratna Bhikku.
...
Hello.

So, do lots of people come to Kushinagar these days?
Will you have chai?
Yes, mostly in the winter season. You have Sri Lankans, Thai, Japanese ... recently the Dalai Lama had also come.
Sure!
Ya!
Kushinagar was first developed by the Venerable Chandramani Mahathera. You know — the Thai Buddhist monk who witnessed the vows during Dr Ambedkar's conversion to Buddhism in 1956. He also started a school and college here.
What about the Buddhist temples?
They were all mostly built during the 1990s, the then Mayawati government also contributed.
Right now I don't see many tourists.
Yes, yes, the season will start soon. You know, we conduct walks for tourists to see all the places where the Buddha spent his last days. Nearby is Pava, where the Buddha had his last meal ...

Where are you staying here?
At Pathik Niwas, the government hotel.

We tried at the Chinese guest house, but they said they don't give rooms to Indians, only to foreigners.

Oh! Yes, that must be because of local youth creating problems. Nowadays people are getting spoiled by liquor, films. There is a local liquor bar just 7-8 km from here, and they hire girls there.

These college students also come here. Nowadays we don't allow them much ... You know, my husband is a brahmin, and I am upper caste, from Nepal, but we treat everyone equal, you know.

Yes, yes, the Buddha said that a man becomes brahmin by his actions and not by birth.

But you know, after reaching a level in spiritual practice, everything is the same, there is no religion ... Gorakhnath also preached the same thing as the Buddha, but through yoga. Today we have Sathya Sai Baba and all ...

?

So where are you from? How did you become a bhikku?
I am actually from Mainpuri district, near Agra. I became a monk when I was eleven years old.

Was it your own decision?

Yes, it was, but I had to ask my parents for permission.

Are there any rituals to follow?

You have to take the ten precepts of the Samanera to be ordained as a novice monk. I am part of the Theravada tradition, like most Indian Buddhists today.

Upali, once Siddhatta Gotama's barber, is said to have recited the monastic code, or Vinaya (Discipline), at the First Buddhist Council held at Rajgriha shortly after the Tathagata's death. This code had been improvised by the Tathagata, who added and changed rules, depending on the situation. As a result of this pragmatic approach, there has been plenty of disagreement over monastic code throughout Buddhist history.

Sanskrit Vinaya manuscript found at Bamiyan, Afghanistan. 4th c. CE.

After the age of nineteen, you can be ordained as a bhikku. There are 227 precepts to follow for that.

Can you become a monk after having been married?

You can, but it is not advisable. After marriage you develop a lot of karmic bonds, and it is difficult to let go of all that.

So what do you do now?
I am now editor of this newspaper.

It is called *Buddha Jyoti*.

Hmm ... published from Allahabad, interesting.
बुद्ध ज्योति

ज्योति
पाक्षिक
गुमनामी के अंधेरे में
अयोध्या-बोतल में बन्द

Oh, you don't know, Nandratna Bhikku is a very important man, he was serving in the UP state government!

Uh ... haan... I was the head of a Buddhist organization, but I gave it up. Too much politics! HAHA!

Kaa
HOLY
HIKING
OSTCARDS
OF KUSHINAGAR
AVAILABLE
TOUR
Kaa

So you come here at 8 tomorrow morning and Nandratna Bhikku can take you around.
AM
FOOD
GIFT
ITE
FREE
TRAVEL
INFORMA

clic!

Ric
Ric
Ric
Ric
Ric
Croak
Ric
Ric
Ric
Ric
Ric
Ric
Ric
Croak
Ric

Oh shit! It's already 7.45! Looks like we're going to be late!

YAMA
Did Nandratna Bhikku come here?

Yes, but he left sometime ago.

प्राचीन कुशीनगर के भग्नावशेष
REMAINS OF ANCIENT KUSHINAGAR
भारतीय पुरातत्व सर्वेक्षण
ARCHAEOLOGICAL SURVEY OF INDIA

The main stupa at Kushinagar marks the spot where the Tathagata died. The site was abandoned for nearly a millennium until excavated and identified by British archaeologist A.C.L.Carlleyle in 1876. When Xuanzang visited it in the seventh century, there used to be monasteries nearby, and a large temple in front of it. In 1927, Burmese Buddhists restored the stupa and the nirvana temple to its present condition.

Let's look around the temple first.

Wow ... it feels so nice and calm here, no?

A little later ...
...
clic!
Which country you are coming?
Take your photos somewhere else, okay! You have no other work or what!
Cool down, it's okay ...
Just can't control my anger! Living the Buddha's teachings takes real effort!

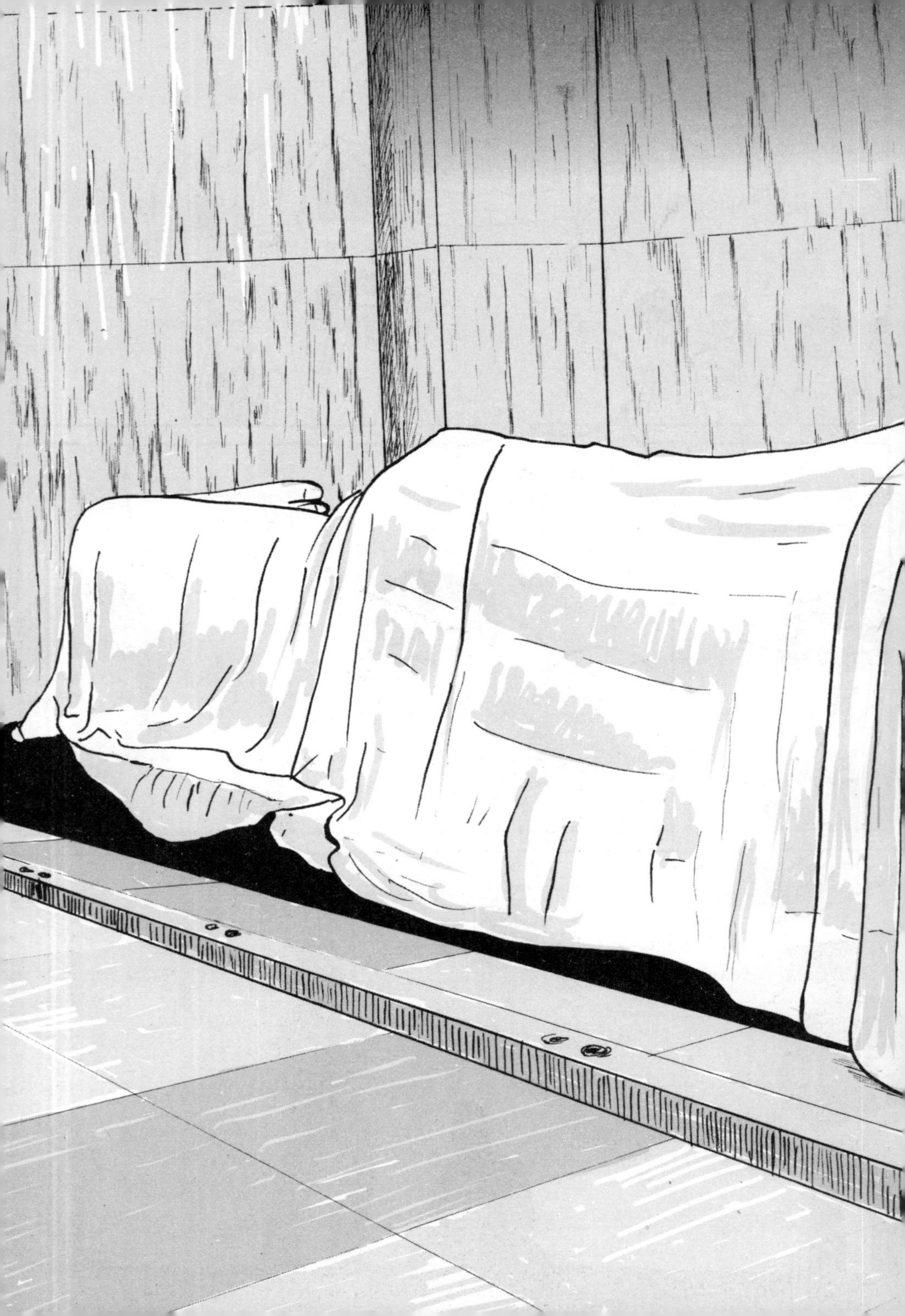

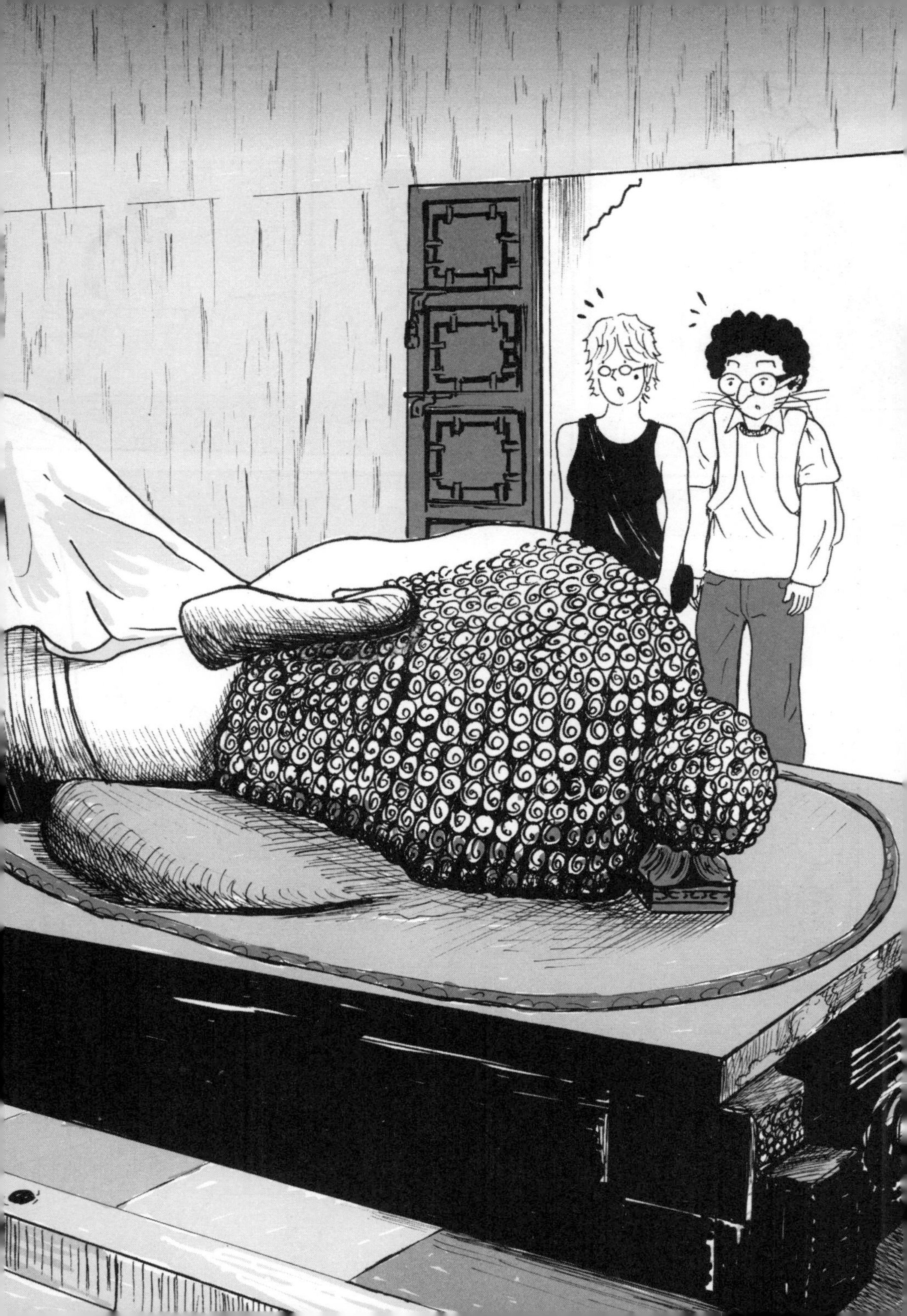

DONATION BOX

This 6.1-metre statue of the Tathagata was carved out of red sandstone in the fifth century, during the Gupta era. It represents the exact position that he is reported to have died in, at this location. There was a grove of sal trees here, outside the town of Kusinara, belonging to the Malla tribe.

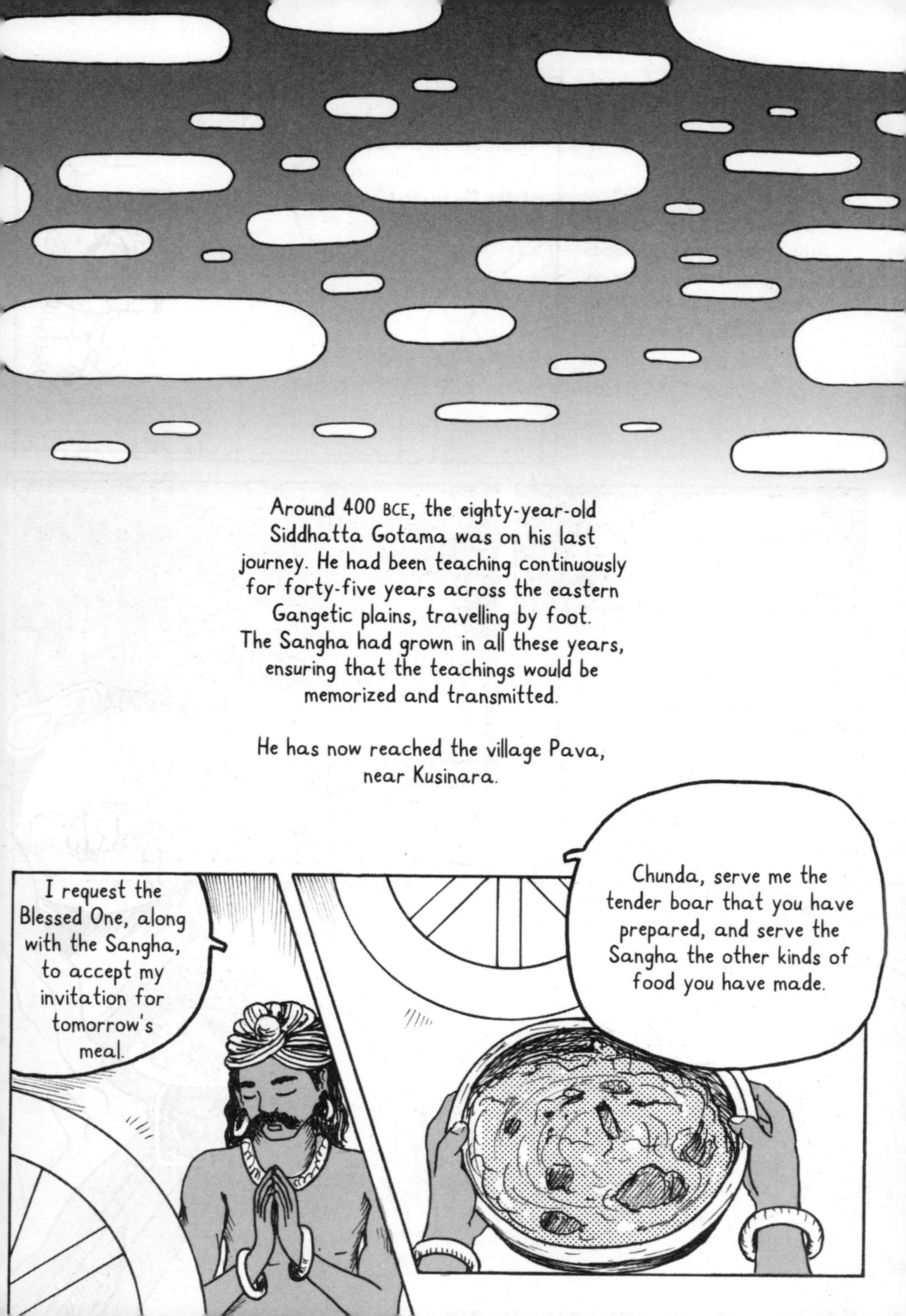
Around 400 BCE, the eighty-year-old Siddhatta Gotama was on his last journey. He had been teaching continuously for forty-five years across the eastern Gangetic plains, travelling by foot. The Sangha had grown in all these years, ensuring that the teachings would be memorized and transmitted.
He has now reached the village Pava, near Kusinara.
I request the Blessed One, along with the Sangha, to accept my invitation for tomorrow's meal.
Chunda, serve me the tender boar that you have prepared, and serve the Sangha the other kinds of food you have made.

The Tathagata fell seriously ill after eating that meal, passing blood in his stools and suffering severe pains as though he were close to death.

Come, Ananda, we shall move on to the further bank of the River Hirannavati, to Upavattana, the sal grove of the Mallas at Kusinara.
Yes, venerable sir!

Ananda, could you prepare a bed for me between two sal trees with the head to the north? I am tired and must lie down.

Bhikku, where is Ananda?
The venerable Ananda is in the monks' dwelling, leaning against the gatepost, weeping.

Go, bhikku, and call Ananda in my name, saying, 'Venerable Ananda, the teacher calls you.'

Enough Ananda! Do not grieve and lament. Have I not warned about this before: we must lose and be deprived of and separated from everything pleasant and dear.
Sniff

How else could it be? That something is born, comes into being, is conditioned, and is of a nature that decays; that it should not decay — this cannot happen. For a long time, Ananda, you have attended on the Tathagata, acting in body, in speech, in thought; kindly, helpfully, gladly, honestly, without limits.

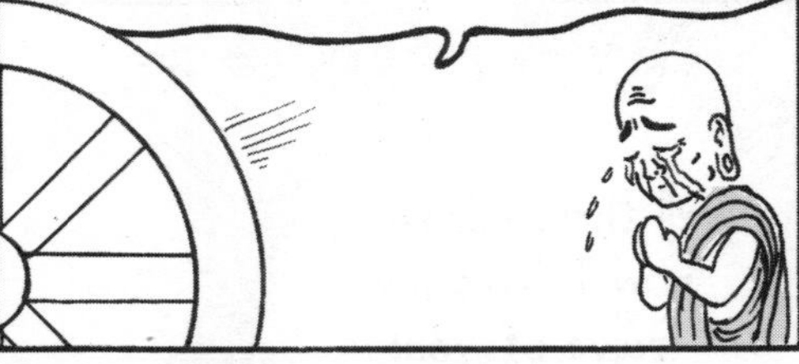

You have made merit, Ananda. Keep on applying yourself and very soon you will be free of the taints ... Ananda, go into Kusinara and tell the Mallas there that tonight, in the last watch, the final nibbana of the Tathagata will happen.

Before passing away, the Pali suttas tell us, the Tathagata gave various instructions about how his funeral should be conducted, the four places of pilgrimage related to his life, tips on monastic life, and he ordained the last convert, Subhadda. He also refused to name a leader of the Sangha, urging the monks to treat the Dhamma as guide instead.

Perhaps one of you has a doubt or is confused about the Buddha, the Dhamma, the Sangha, the path or the practice. Ask your questions, bhikkus. Do not later regret that, although your teacher was right in front of you, you were not able to put your questions to the Blessed One.
Perhaps you do not ask your questions out of respect for the teacher. Let one companion tell another his questions.
Well then, bhikkhus, now I take my leave of you: vayadhamma samkhara appamadena sampadeta!
'It is the nature of conditioned things to decay. If you are attentive, you will succeed.'
These were the last words of the Tathagata.

Krackle
Kaa Kaa
Krackle
The Tathagata's cremated remains, after some deliberation, were distributed into eight equal portions among the claimants. They were then carried to various territories, and, with the relic urns buried underneath, stupas were built over them.

Elephant carrying the Buddha's relics. Relief from Bharhut, 2nd c. BCE, National Museum, Delhi.

कृपया स्तूप
पर न चढ़ें

This is the site of the Tathagata's cremation, locally known as Ramabhar, after a nearby pond. The mound was exposed in 1910, and later identified as the stupa built on the cremation site. The stupa has been built over many times, the latest being from the fifth century CE.

रामाभार स्तूप के उत्तरवनित अवशेष
EXCAVATED REMAINS OF RAMABHAR STUPA

Give us something for tea ...

clic!

It's beautiful. Let's sit here for a while.

Old wrought-iron benches ... surely from the British era.

Plotch!
I think it's time to leave.

The locals called a large seated stone figure at this location Matha-Kuar, which was found to be a Buddha idol. It was this site that led Alexander Cunningham to identify these ruins as ancient Kusinara. Monsoon water had flooded the place when we visited.

clic!

Oh!
Kutch!

Bharath! The lens cap has fallen in the mud! Please take it out, no?

...

Ya, okay, coming.

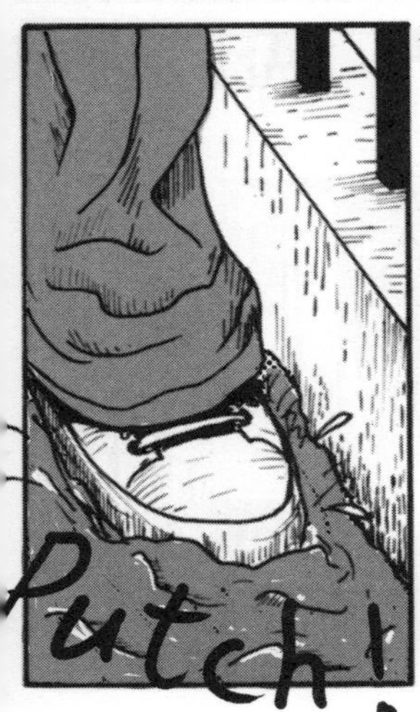
Putch!

Take us to Yama Cafe.

Srr
Srr

CAFE
DELIC
FOO
GIFT
ITEM
FREE
TRAVEL
INFORMA

Ah! Really needed the lemon tea.

Hello! Enjoying? Did you see the stupas?

It was amazing! Very calm and peaceful.

AMA CAFE

Hello, Roy, how are you doing?
Oh, Suresh, I am fine. Let me introduce you to some nice people.

Hello, I'm Suresh Ramachandran.

Hi, I'm Bharath, and this is Alka.

The usual for me ... one veg soup and a veg chowmein.

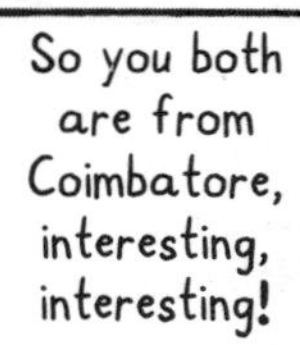

So you both are from Coimbatore, interesting, interesting!

Ya, that's where we live right now. So where are you from?

See, I am Tamil, born and brought up in Singapore, but now I live in Australia. It's really nice to meet a Tamil speaker here, in Kushinagar!

So what brings you here?

You see, I became a Buddhist a few years ago and this is the first time I am making a pilgrimage to the four main spots. Are you people Buddhists too?

Yes, we became Buddhists recently. May I ask what made you choose Buddhism?
Well, when I was about twelve or thirteen years old, I started questioning the Hindu gods ... But it all started ... See, I was a big fan of MGR, you know, the film actor and ex-chief minister of Tamil Nadu.

In Singapore, there used to be fights between the MGR fan clubs and those of his rival film star Sivaji Ganesan. I was attracted to MGR because he was a helper, a giver, a social reformer. But later I found that he was also an egotist and megalomaniac.
MGR
SIVAJI GANESAN

Because Periyar was the guru of the Dravidian movement, I started reading about his ideologies. I liked his atheism.

E.V.Ramaswamy (1879–1973), better known as 'Periyar', began the Dravidian Movement in the 1930s after quitting the Congress party, which he said served only the interests of the brahmins. He preached the principles of self-respect, rationalism, women's rights, eradication of caste, and the right of the Dravidian people to self-determination.

கடவுளை மற, மனிதனை நினை.
Forget about God, think about man.

Periyar said that this had been said centuries ago by the Buddha.
I am not sure the Buddha actually said something to that effect ...

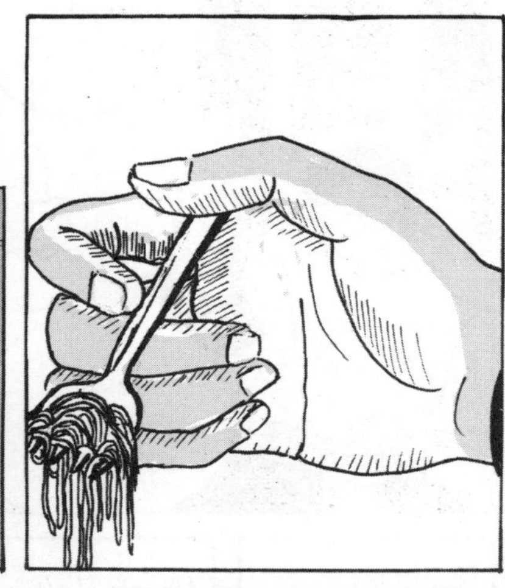

Uh ... Is your family also Buddhist?
No. Only me. My principle is not to force or try to persuade anyone. My wife, she's okay with it, you know.

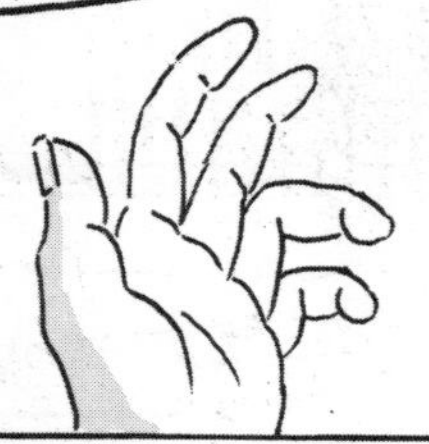
I have a small meditation room in the backyard of my house in Melbourne.

After coming back from my day job as an accountant, I meditate there.

Everything going fine?
Yes, Roy. Why don't you join us?

Your hotel is comfortable?
Oh yes. It is expensive, but very comfortable.

Where do you stay, Roy?

Oh, we stay close by. We bought some land here when we came, and slowly built a house.

At the end of the road from here, there is a Hindu village, a Muslim village, a 'mixed' village and a brahmin village. Our land is in the brahmin village. We also adopted two kids.

YAMA CAFE
One of the kids, a girl, was found abandoned nearby. We took her in because no one came to claim the baby. There are many interesting stories like this here ... Ha ha! You know, a miracle happened to me once!

Once, I got a relic, you know. You know what a relic is, no? Small container with some remains of holy monks, arahats, you know.

But how do you know if it's authentic?

It was given to me by a Thai monk, and it was the cause of the miracle!

I was meditating one day when I felt like someone was sitting next to me. When I looked, the Sathya Sai Baba picture next to me glowed!

It must be because of Sathya Sai Baba's powers, because when I opened my eyes ...

... the relic container multiplied and became four!

...
...
? ?

YAMA
Um ... I think we'll leave now ... See you, Suresh, it was nice talking to you ...

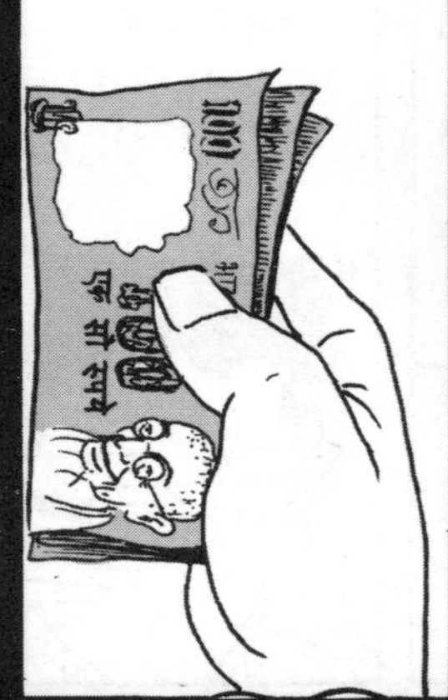

In his mind, the Buddha, Sai Baba, Gorakhnath all seem to be mixed up into one big spiritual dish.

YAMA CAFE

Kaa Kaa

A lot of people seem to be confused about the Buddha's teachi — Oh shit! The electricity's gone!

We need to buy a torch; this darkness is so scary!

You will get jeeps at Kasia.
Gorakhpur! Gorakhpur!
Thoo!
UP53 2431
Dryyyyyrrrr...

3.
Marker Stone

Brrrrrrrr
DHAD
We'll soon be at the Nepal border. They will check your luggage.
The Ayodhya verdict is tomorrow, so there's more security now.
Two to three weeks ago, they seized some guns in a truck.
They check with dogs at the border!
Brrrr

Brrr

What's in the bag?

Where are you going?
Lumbini.

Take down the suitcase.

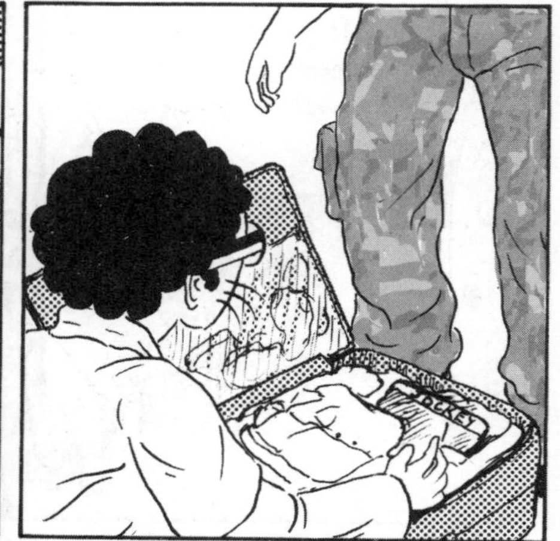

Okay, move ahead.

Now there will be two more checkpoints.
Brrr
I didn't see any dogs though ...
STOP

भारत सीमा समाप्त
INDIAN BORDER ENDS
NEPAL
The border is ahead. You can take a rickshaw across.

If you have a camera, show it to the customs people ...

... and don't pay them more than fifty rupees.

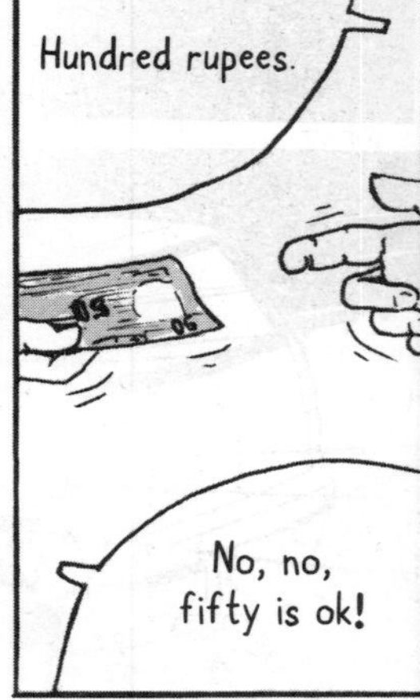
Hundred rupees.
No, no, fifty is ok!

WELCOME TO INDIA
Hundred rupees.
Hundred rupees? We didn't even cover hundred metres!
But I saved you fifty rupees at the customs!
How much longer to Lumbini?
From the border, about an hour's drive.
These roads are mostly unpaved. You can hardly see through the dust!
TATA
Indica
Kutch
Kutch
Brrrr...

The Korean monastery didn't take you in? Let's go to Lumbini village, just 3 km away. There are good hotels there.
Will we get food there at this late hour?
Yes you will ...
Lumbini Village L
BY
WELCOME
Lum
Village
He will show you room on third floor, madam.
Okay ... um, what is your name?
Jupiter. That's what everyone calls me here. Hehe ...
Hmm ... nice place!
What can we get to eat right now?
Now ... you will get chicken curry and rice.
Wow! A mango tree in the middle of the courtyard.

Here are the cycles.
Please come back in the evening by five. Enjoy your day!
Okay, thanks, Jupiter!
OUCH!
Srr
careful!
लुम्बिनी भिडियो सेन्टर
VCR
Srr Srr

TAK
MAYADEVI ENTRANCE GA
WELCOME
Oh! A snail ...
clic
भगवान शाक्यमुनि बुद्धको जन्म-स्थल
(मायादेवी मन्दिर, लुम्बिनी, नेपाल)
THE BIRTH PLACE OF SHAKYAMUNI BUDDHA
MAYADEVI TEMPLE, LUMBINI, NEPAL
All of this looks so ordinary, like something hastily set up for tourists. The Mayadevi temple itself looks weird — like a warehouse!

Lumbini was among the last sites related to the life of Siddhatta Gotama to be rediscovered. Dr Alois Anton Fuhrer, a former Catholic priest and archaeologist with the British Indian government, and local prince Khadga Shumsher Rana found it half-buried in the ground in December 1896. Proper excavation began three years later, revealing monastic ruins.

Ashoka visited Lumbini circa 250 BCE and a commemorative stone pillar was erected to mark the site. An inscription by local ruler Ripu Malla, from the fourteenth century, shows that Lumbini was active as a pilgrimage site up until then.

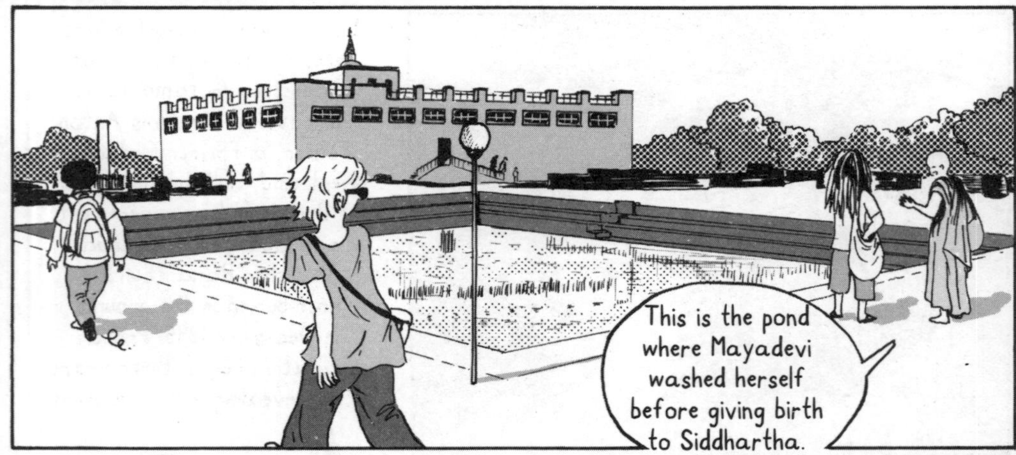
This is the pond where Mayadevi washed herself before giving birth to Siddhartha.

Ah! There's the Ashoka inscription!
'King Piyadassi (Ashoka), the beloved of the gods, in the twentieth year of his reign, himself made a royal visit. Sakyamuni Buddha was born here, therefore the (birth spot) marker stone was worshipped and a stone pillar was erected. The lord having been born here, the tax of Lumbini village is reduced to the eighth part (only).'
The Ashokan inscriptions in the eastern Ganga plains, like this one, use Magahi, the court language of the Mauryan empire. Siddhatta Gotama is thought to have spoken a dialect of this language.

I'm going to light one of those candles ...
Oh. I don't have a match!
Uh, do you have a matchbox?
Yes.
CATS
Thanks.
CATS
Fric
दियो तथा मैनबती बाल्ने

?
Huh! This place is not a working temple at all, it's a museum to house the ruins!

A stone marking the birthplace of the Tathagata! Wow!
...

भगवान बुद्ध जन्म स्मारक शिला
MARKER STONE
The Exact BirthPlace of Buddha

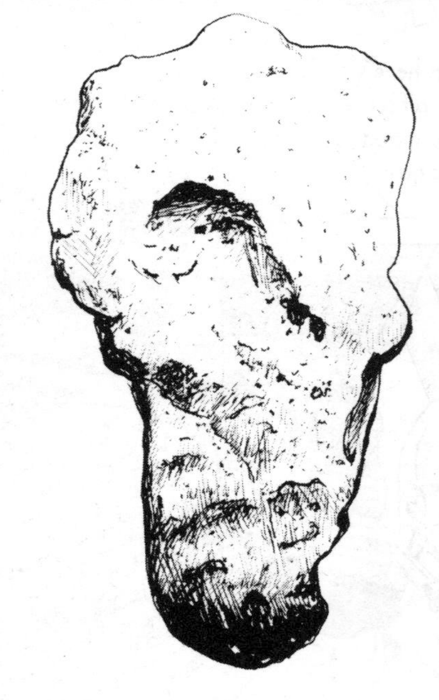

This stone was discovered during excavations in 1996, buried under layers of bricks. Its identification as marking the birthplace is based on its position in the temple and the interpretation of one word from the Ashokan inscription 'silavigadabhica', which is now translated as marker stone.

It's better here, you know, after the sombre mood in Kushinagar.
Ya ...

So shall we go see the museum? It's close by, I think.
Okay.

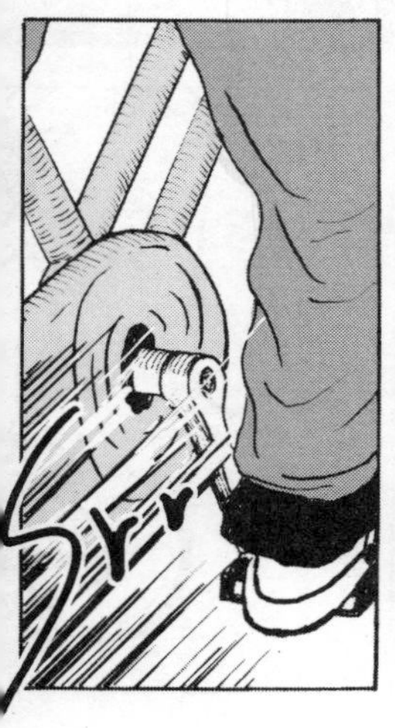

A huge modern complex still under construction, with international monasteries on either side ...

Have we reached yet?

I asked those fishing guys, it's that building right there.

Oho! It's all so muddy here! Looks like we are behind the museum.

...

That calf!
It's fallen
into the pond!
plut plut
Splotch!

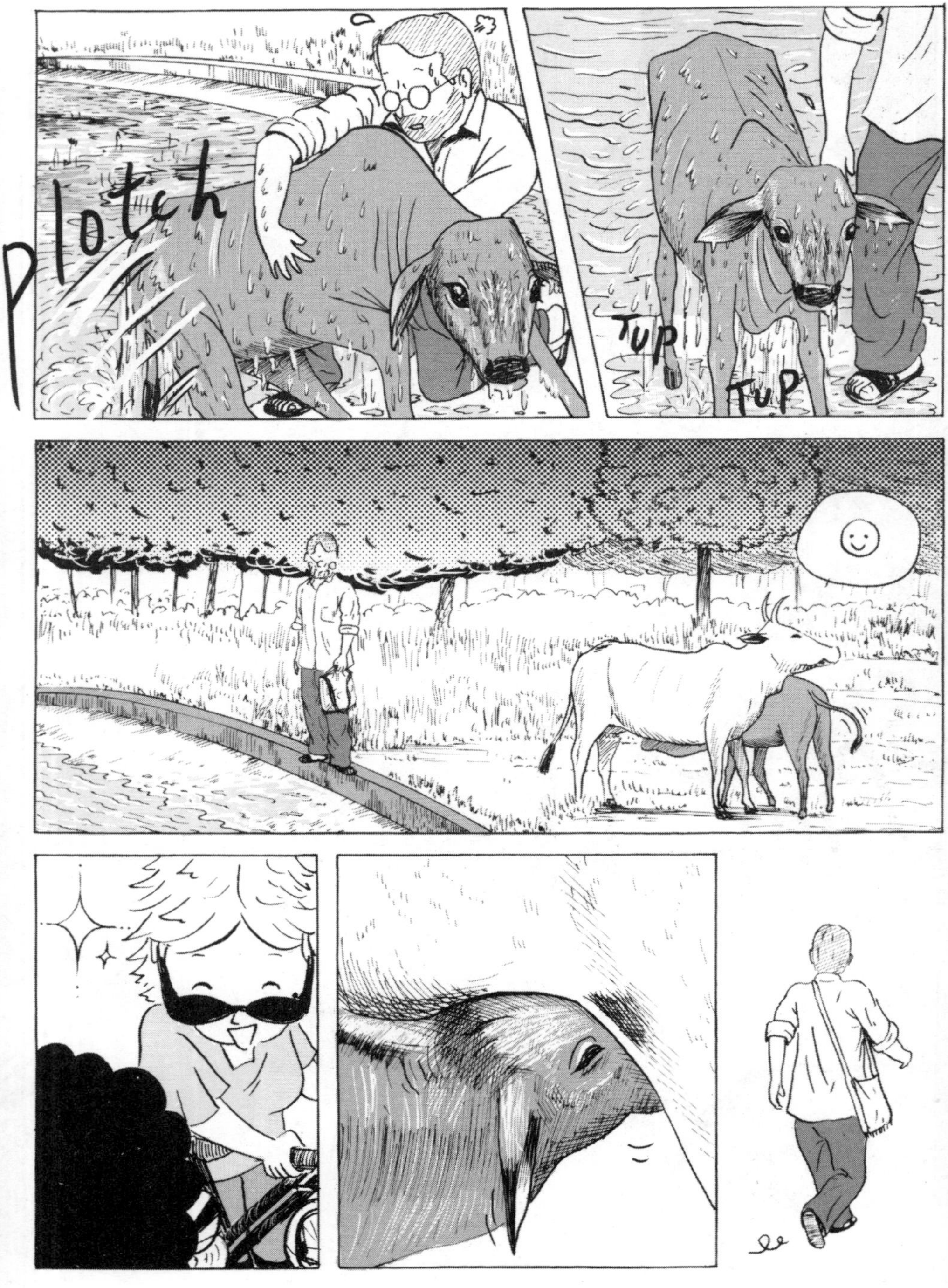

Plotch

TUP
TUP

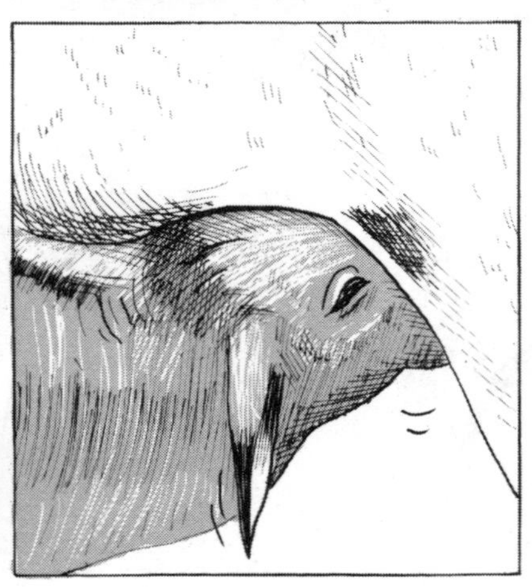

Lumbini Village Lo
Lumbi
Village Lo

Hello!
NEPAL

Hello ... uh, is Jupiter there?

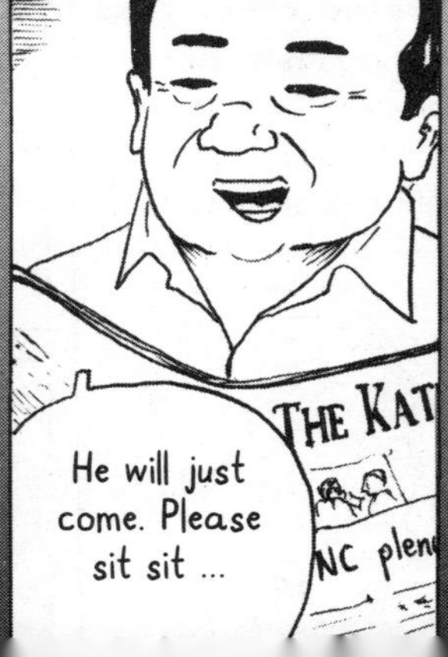
He will just come. Please sit sit ...
THE KAT

You are from India?
Yes.

EPAL
From Delhi?
How did he know?
Yes.

I've lived in Delhi. I was working there for some time. Then I moved to Australia ... but originally from Nepal.

Ah ... Australia. What were you doing there?

I was working in construction ... I'm an architect.

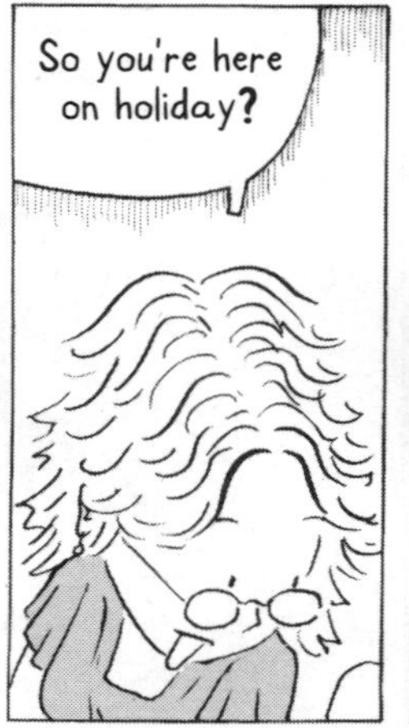
So you're here on holiday?

No, no, actually I'm on business. I'm working on a project here.

We are building one of the monasteries in the Lumbini monastic zone, which was created by Kenzo Tange, the Japanese architect. United Nations has helped develop the place.

We're just coming from the monastic area. Some of the monastic buildings are quite well ornamented!

Well ... it's good work. But, you know, it's not easy to get work in Nepal. I came because I wanted to start something here.

India is a growing economy, there must be lot of opportun—

Welcome to Lumbini Village Lodge
—there's Jupiter.

You from South Korea, yes?
Yes.

You can go to room number 203, second floor. I will come.

Okay, I'll go now ... nice meeting you!
See you!

KATHMANDU POST
NC plenum message: Unity essential
The most favoured

Wonder what happened with the Ayodhya verdict ...

Oh, it's yesterday's newspaper.
POST

Do you have today's paper?

Uh ... no. You want to know about the Ayodhya verdict?
Ya.
The land has been divided into three parts, two for Hindu groups and one for Muslims.

Any violence reported?
No, I don't think.
How did he read my mind?

So you've arranged the car for Tilaurakot tomorrow, right?

Oh yes yes, I will confirm it now. Just wait ... Hello?... Haan! ... Gaadi ...

I really enjoyed Lumbini.
Me too!

SHIT! Lights gone again!
Oh, never mind.

KISS

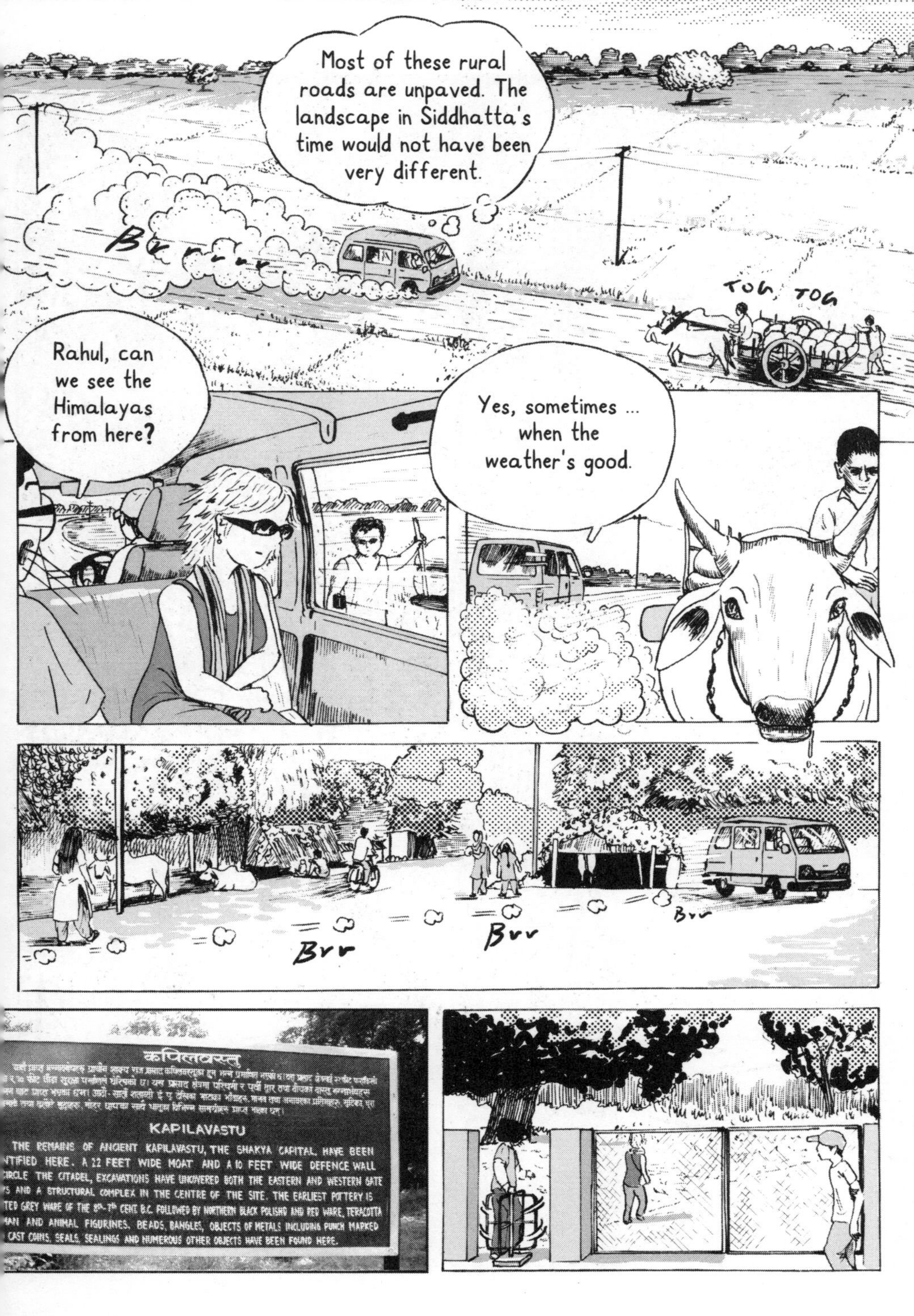

Most of these rural roads are unpaved. The landscape in Siddhatta's time would not have been very different.
Brrrrr
TOG, TOG
Rahul, can we see the Himalayas from here?
Yes, sometimes ... when the weather's good.
Brr
Brr
Brr
कपिलवस्तु
KAPILAVASTU
THE REMAINS OF ANCIENT KAPILAVASTU, THE SHAKYA CAPITAL, HAVE BEEN
NTIFIED HERE. A 22 FEET WIDE MOAT AND A 10 FEET WIDE DEFENCE WALL
IRCLE THE CITADEL, EXCAVATIONS HAVE UNCOVERED BOTH THE EASTERN AND WESTERN GATE
S AND A STRUCTURAL COMPLEX IN THE CENTRE OF THE SITE. THE EARLIEST POTTERY IS
TED GREY WARE OF THE 8th-7th CENT. B.C. FOLLOWED BY NORTHERN BLACK POLISHD AND RED WARE, TERACOTTA
IAN AND ANIMAL FIGURINES. BEADS, BANGLES, OBJECTS OF METALS INCLUDING PUNCH MARKED
CAST COINS, SEALS, SEALINGS AND NUMEROUS OTHER OBJECTS HAVE BEEN FOUND HERE.

The western gateway. These remains must be from after the Tathāgata's death. Kiln-fired bricks were not in use during his time.
This is an abandoned forest out here!
Ya, abandoned even when Fa Xien visited in about 400 CE.
But there's another site that the Indian side claims as Kapilavastu, right?
From what I read, most people agree this is the site. There are also more remains here.

Hey, check this out! A really long earthworm!

पूर्वी द्वार
"महाभिनिष्क्रमण द्वार" को नामले प्रसिद्ध यस द्वारबाट भगवान
जीवन त्याग गर्नु भएको थियो। उत्खननबाट २९ फीट चौंडा बाटो
जस्ता वास्तु अवशेषकासाथै माटाका मानव र जनावरका प्रतिमाहरु
र ब्राह्मी अभिलेखयुक्त मोहर छाप प्राप्त भएका छन्।
EASTERN GATE WAY
THE EASTERN GATE WAY ALSO KNOWN AS "MAHĀBHINISHKRAMANA DWĀRA
WHICH LORD BUDDHA LEFT HIS WORLDY LIFE - THIS GATE COMPLEX
WAY FLANKED ON EITHER SIDES BY BASTIONS - OBJECTS FOUND IN THE
HUMAN AND ANIMAL FIGURINES, COINS, BEADS, BENGLES, A SEAL WITH A BRAHMI
WELLA SHERDS OF PAINTED GREY AND NORTHERN BLACK POLISHED WARE

It is unlikely that Siddhatta Gotama left home without the knowledge of his family. He was twenty-nine years old, married and a son had just been born.

He must have thought long and hard about it. Perhaps the birth of Rahula hastened his decision.

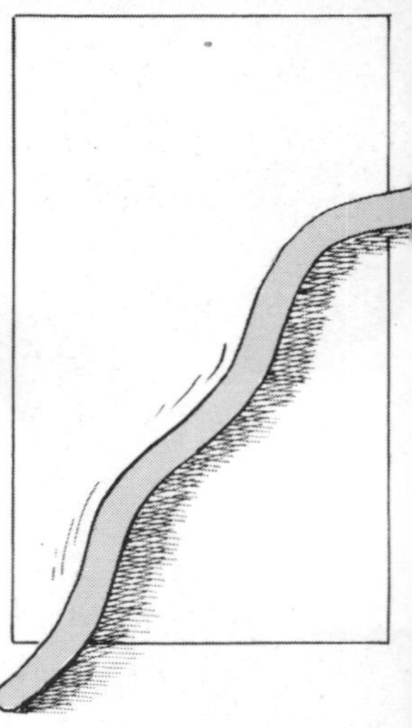

The discovery and identification of the Kapilavastu remains is based on the unearthing of an Ashoka pillar nearby in 1895. These remains were found in 1899 next to a village named Tilaurakot.

An ancient well ...
Let's go see the other side.

Oh!

A temple for a local Hindu goddess ...

... but somehow these cute elephants remind me of the mystical dream of Siddhatta's mother, Maya. According to Buddhist mythology, she dreamt of a white elephant carrying a lotus and entering her womb before her pregnancy. Mayadevi died soon after giving birth to Siddhatta.

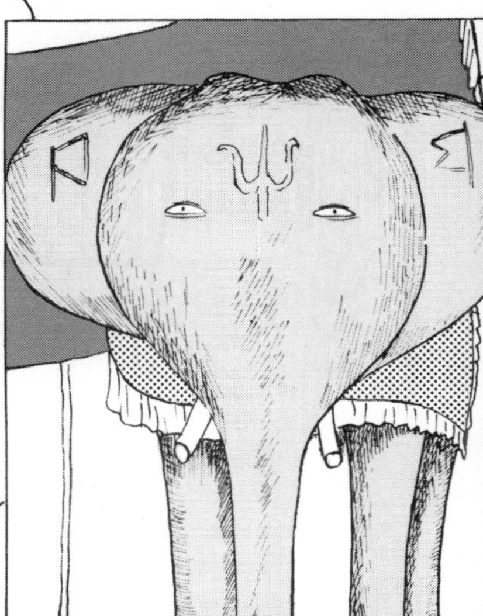

Now we go to Kudan, right?
Yes. It is only half an hour's drive from here.
Drrr...
I need to ask someone ...
Brrr...
Looks like we're going to the Ashoka pillar first.

It's just a little shed in the middle of a rice field.

By Ashoka's time, memorials to previous Buddhas were already a tradition. That's what this pillar indicates.

'King Piyadassi, beloved of the gods, having been anointed fourteen years, increased for the second time the stupa of the Buddha Konakamana, and having been anointed (twenty years) he came himself and worshipped (and) he (caused) this stone.'

Madam, now Kudan?
Yes, let's go.
Vrooo...

This is Kudan?
Yes, sir, this is it.
The place is deserted!

This mound has not even been excavated! Most probably a stupa, but what is that structure on top?

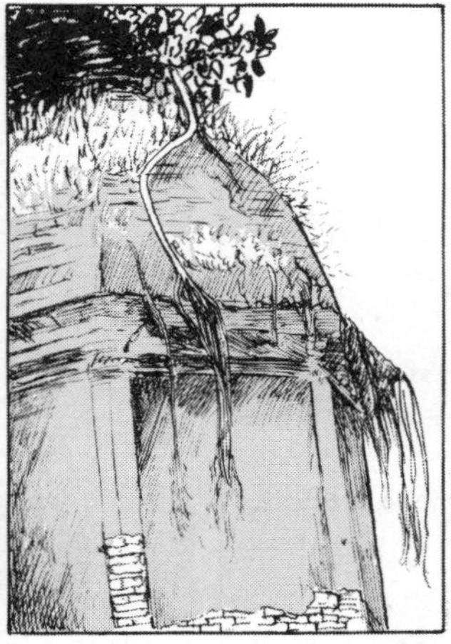

It's a Hindu shrine. Looks relatively recent, but it is abandoned.

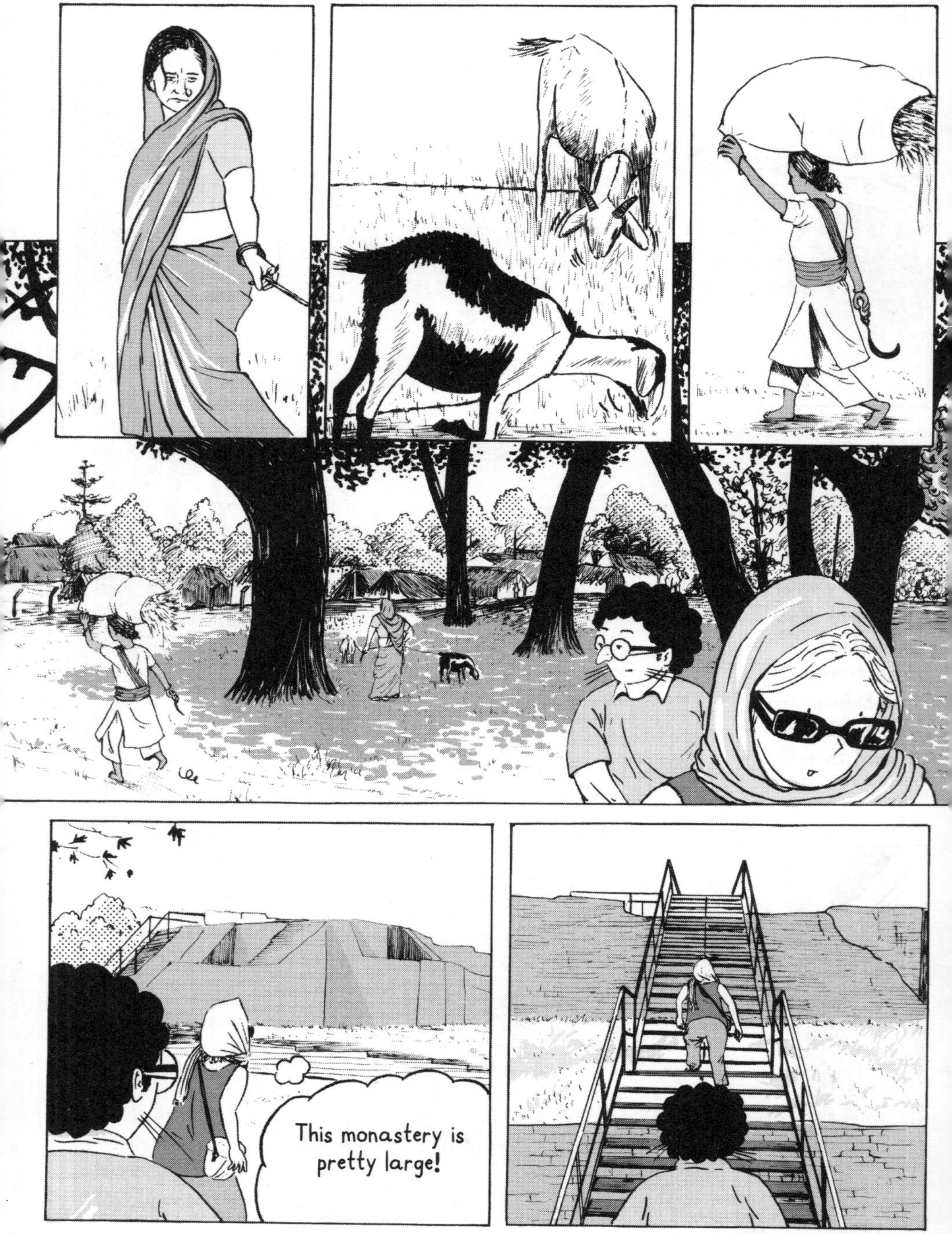

This monastery is
pretty large!

Oh! A Shivalinga on top of a Buddhist vihara ... a rare sight. It's broken though.
...

This is the first direct evidence we see of the appropriation of a Buddhist structure for non-Buddhist purposes.

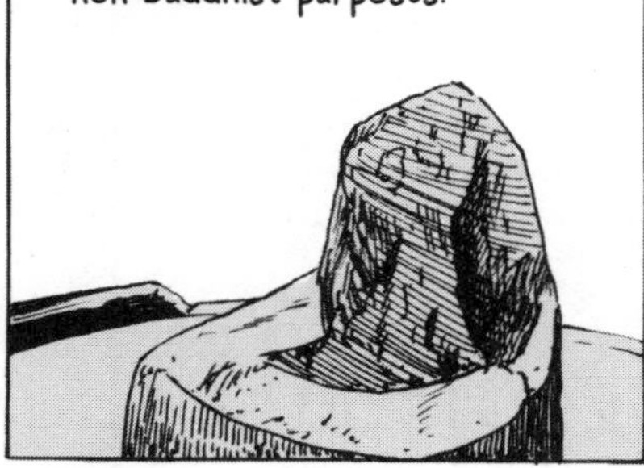

These ruins have been identified as Nigrodharama, the place where the Tathagata first met his father on returning after his Awakening. It was also here that the Tathagata, reluctantly at first, began the bhikkuni (nuns) order at the request of his aunt who wished to enter the Sangha.

WASH!
Hey, wake up Bharath. It's already 6.30 in the evening!
I'll just go out and get some money from the ATM. You be at the reception.
Okay.
Lumbini Village Lodge
Hello madam, how are you? Enjoyed your trip to Kudan?
Oh ya! It was good!
Madam, your name?
Alka.
Alka ... surname?
Singh, Alka Singh.

So I will prepare the bill for you, okay?

Madam, are you kshatriya ... are you from Delhi?

Actually, I am from Bihar. I have never lived there but my parents are from a place called Sitamarhi. I was born and brought up in Delhi.

You know Sitamarhi? It's close to the Nepal border.

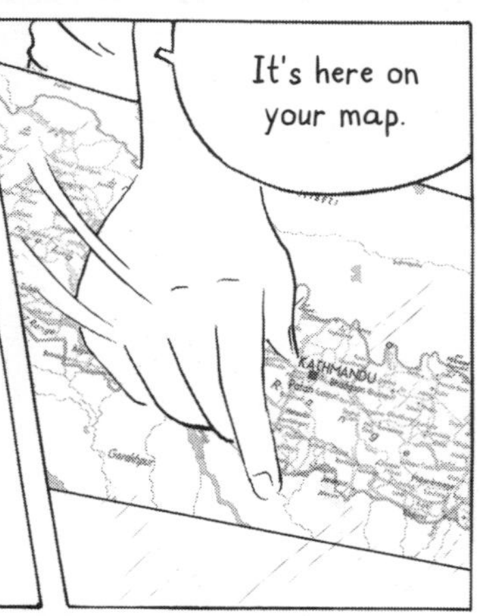

It's here on your map.
KATHMANDU

Oh, okay, okay! Your parents are from here! Very good. But are you kshatriya?

Uh, well ... I am not Hindu actually, I'm a practising Buddhist and I don't really agree with the caste system, so I won't tell you what caste I was given.
Oh

But my parents, through their ancestry, have been landowners.
Oh.
Oh, okay.

So why did you convert? Is your friend also Buddhist?

That's a long story ... he's my husband and, yes, he's also Buddhist.

Essentially, I dislike the Hindu caste system as it is extremely discriminative.

I find the Buddha's teachings very simple and scientific. I agree with everything he has to say. So I converted.

Oh yes, okay ... I also agree with the teachings. I have done vipassana meditation course also.

Actually, I never thought of converting. I don't want to...

Truly speaking, my wife and I, we want to just leave everything and go somewhere else. We are really tired of this place.
Hello! We were just talking about you. Your bill is done.
WAAA! Nepal has turned out to be so expensive!

गोरखपुर ↑ 103 कि मी.
कुशीनगर ↑ 155 कि मी.
सारनाथ ↑ 315 कि मी.
वाराणसी ↑ 318 कि मी.
भारत आगमन पर
आपका हार्दिक स्वागत है।
प्रान्तीय खण्ड लो. नि. वि.
सिद्धार्थनगर
सिद्धार्थनगर ↑ 25 किमी.
बस्ती ↑ 97 किमी.
श्रावस्ती ↑ 154 किमी.
लखनऊ ↑ 295 किमी.

The other car is waiting for us.

Open your bag. Are you Nepali?
No.

You see, Nepalis get girls across the border to work in India, so there's checking.

4.
Fruits of Action

A gigantic Buddha statue in the middle of nowhere! That must be Shravasti.

TOURIST BUNGALOW
SRAVASTI

Cool! We reached in three hours.

What is
your name?

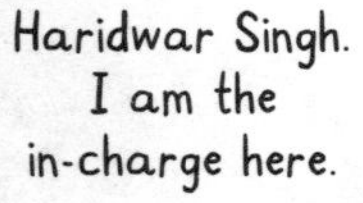
Haridwar Singh.
I am the
in-charge here.

Food will be served
at 7 p.m. in the
dining hall.

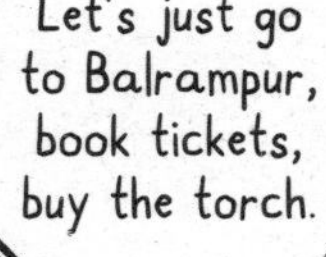

No electricity
for six hours!
Phoo!!
Let's just go
to Balrampur,
book tickets,
buy the torch.
TIC

Drrr
Shravasti! Get down, Shravasti!
Kaaaank
clic
TOURIST BUNGALOW
SHRAVASTI
Did you get the tickets?
Yes, no trouble!

Your name?
Joginder.
Is the food okay, sir?
Yes, it's good.
Are we the only ones in this guest house?
No sir, an MLA is coming — for the panchayat committee elections.
Who?
Srivastav ... he is getting someone to fight his election.
?
Um, it's like this ... I am a Harijan, and I am asked to fight the election for someone else ... right, sir?
Harijan — the word is still used?

Who is fighting the election for Srivastav?

Paswan.

Uh, just wanted to ask, are you Buddhist?

Yes, Buddhist...

RIC

RIC
RIC
RIC
RIC
RIC

UP TOU
SRAV

A Jain temple right next to the guest house.

Mahavira (Nigantha Nataputta in the Pali suttas), founder of the Jain tradition, was a contemporary of the Tathagata.

Mahavira died before the Tathagata, near Nalanda.

INTERNAL ROAD SHRAVASTI
DISTRICT BAHRAICH
WAS INAUGURATED
ON SEPTEMBER 30 1995 SATURDAY
BY
HON.BLE Ms. MAYAWATI
M. IFTAKHARUDDIN
DISTRICT MAGISTR
BAHRAICH
Both were teaching in the same areas, so most Buddhist sites are also Jain pilgrimage sites. But it is not known if they met each other.

Will you show us around?
Sure, please sit.
786

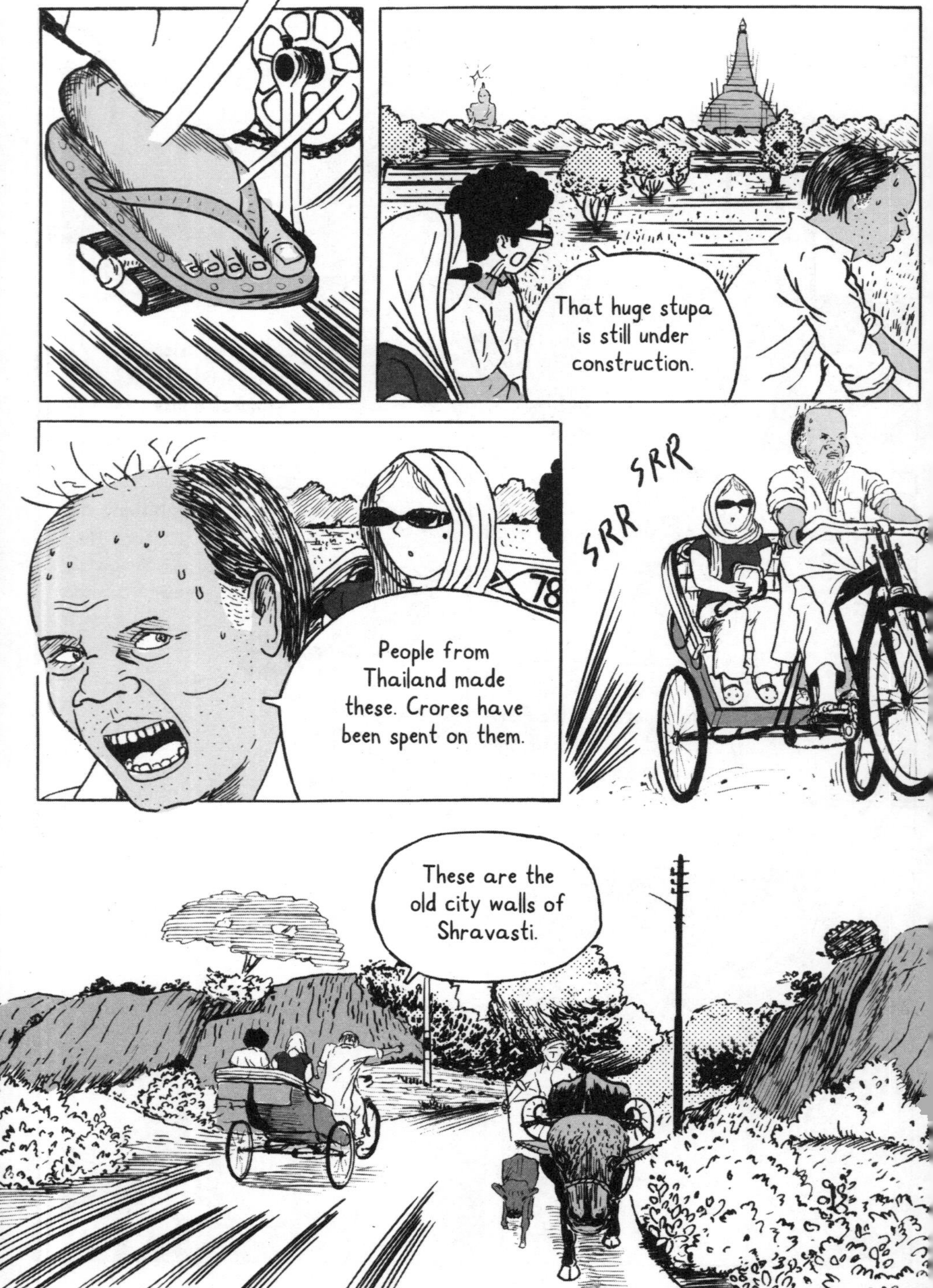
That huge stupa is still under construction.
People from Thailand made these. Crores have been spent on them.
78
SRR
SRR
These are the old city walls of Shravasti.

First you can see the Jain temple.
Jainism and Buddhism are related and yet so different.
Both have similar iconographies, monastic orders, do not believe in a creator god, are part of the same non-brahminical shramana tradition.
And yet, Mahavira taught the existence of an eternal soul (atman), while the Tathagata taught its non-existence.
Mughal-era structure built over the temple, just like the one in Sarnath.

'I have heard that on one occasion the Blessed One was staying near Savatthi in Jeta's grove, Anathapindika's monastery.' So begin the maximum number of Pali suttas, as it is here that the Tathagata spent twenty-five monsoon retreats, more than in any other place. Savatthi, the capital of the Kosala kingdom, was ruled by king Pasenadi, who became a Buddhist.
There are two stupas here, Angulimala and Sudatta.

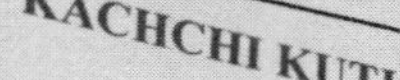

KACHCHI KUTI
the most important excavated s
in Maheth. It is identified w
of Sudatta popularly kno
indika as referred by the
travelers Fa-Hien and Hi
FFFF

Sudatta was a rich banker (setthi) from Savatthi. He came across a young, newly awakened Siddhatta on one of his business trips to Rajgriha, the Magadhan capital, and invited him to Savatthi. Here, on land he bought outside the city, Sudatta built for the Sangha its first-ever monastery. As an influential supporter of the Sangha from its beginning, he became known as Anathapindika (feeder of the destitute) and this stupa was dedicated to him.

The Tathagata taught some of his most profound doctrines at Savatthi, but his life was surrounded by intrigue and controversy.
Apparently, he was challenged to perform a miracle to silence a rival group, even though he had spoken against such gimmicks.
Ya ... and then there was the lengthy politics between Kosala and Sakya, leading to a violent invasion of his own people by Kosala.
The Pali suttas also mention attempts to discredit the Tathagata by spreading a rumour about a woman who was found dead near his hut. They said she visited him often at night.
All this scandal seems so familiar today.

The stupa dedicated to Angulimala,
the murderer-turned-monk,
was an even more impressive affair.
Wow! Look how high the ceiling is! This building seems to have had more than a ceremonial purpose.
Ah! A covered passageway.
Here's the entrance.

...
Do not take this road, samana! On this road is Angulimala, the murderer. He has killed many and wears their fingers as a garland.
?

STOP!
Humph!
Samana! I said STOP!

I have stopped, Angulimala, you stop too.
SURRR
These samanas, sons of the Sakyans, speak only the truth. But though this samana is still walking, he says he has stopped.
Even as you walk, samana, you tell me you have stopped. I ask you now, samana, how is it that you have stopped and I have not?

Angulimala, I have stopped forever. I abstain from violence towards living beings, but you have no such restraint. That is why I have stopped and you have not.
!

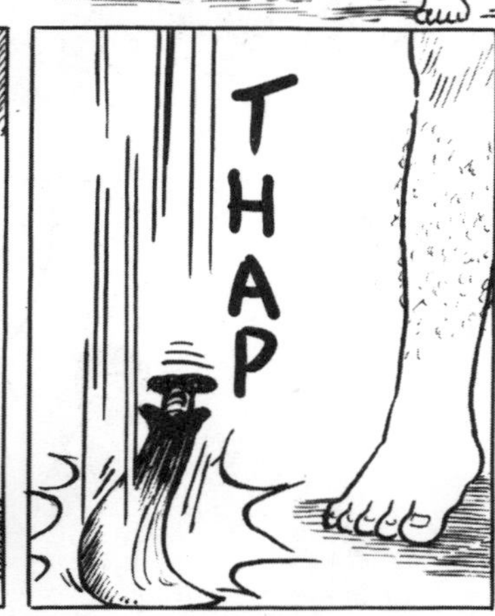

THAP

*Ehi bhikku! Come, monk!

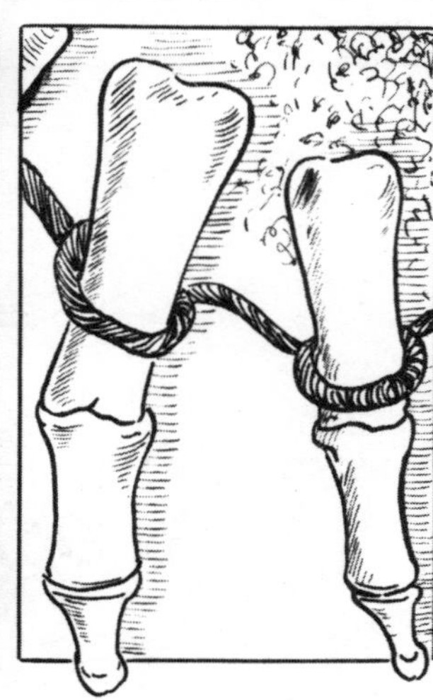

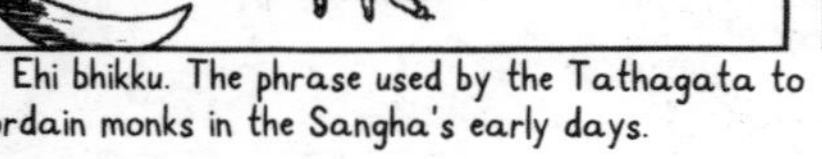
* Ehi bhikku. The phrase used by the Tathagata to ordain monks in the Sangha's early days.

The Pali commentaries say that Angulimala was of high birth and that these fingers were demanded by his teacher whose wrath he had incurred. The Vinaya records that some people accused the Tathagata of using the Sangha as a sanctuary for criminals. This led the Tathagata to proclaim the rule that criminals should not be ordained. The scholar Richard Gombrich has suggested that he might have been part of a ritual cult.
Okay, let's go to Jetavana.
S-V-V-S-V-V

These kids don't go to school?
They go ... there is one in the market, a private school.
Is it good?
It's okay. You see that building there?
That's the government school which gets flooded every monsoon. So it's closed most of the time.
Svv Svv
Is it still under water?
Yes, it's closed right now.
Svv Svv
Jetavana ... you have to buy a ticket to go in.

Anathapindika bought this park as a rainy season retreat for the Sangha, at a great cost. The story goes that he was challenged by Jeta, prince and owner of the land, to take as much land as could be covered by his wealth of gold coins. This event has been a popular subject for representation in Buddhist art.

Listen and pay
close attention.
I will speak.

There are these five facts that one should reflect on often, whether one is a woman or a man, lay or ordained. Which five?
'I am subject to ageing, have not gone beyond ageing.' This is the first fact that one should reflect on often, whether one is a woman or a man, lay or ordained.

'I am subject to illness, have not gone beyond illness. I am subject to death, have not gone beyond death. I will grow different, separate from all that is dear and appealing to me.'

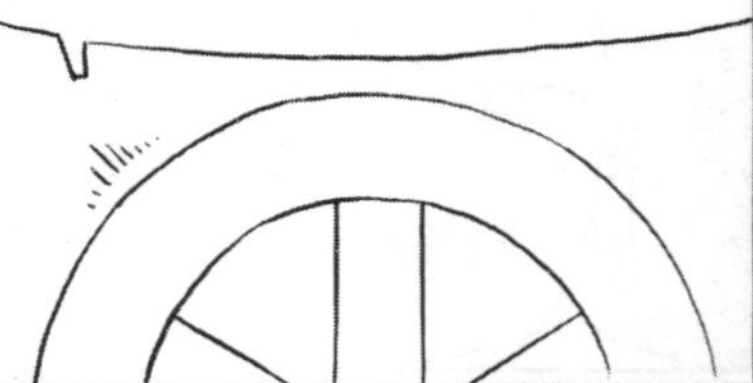

'I am the owner of my actions, heir to my actions, born of my actions, related through my actions, and have my actions as my arbitrator.'

'Whatever I do, for good or for evil, to that I will fall heir.'

These are the five facts that one should reflect on often, whether one is a woman or a man, lay or ordained.

Venerable sir, in the morning I dressed and, taking my bowl and outer robe, went into Savatthi for alms.

As I was wandering for alms from house to house, I saw a certain woman giving birth to a deformed child. When I saw that, I thought, 'Indeed, how beings are afflicted!'
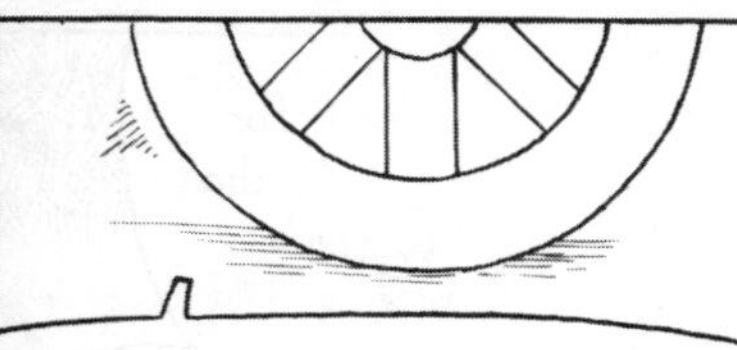
In that case, Angulimala, go into Savatthi and say to that woman, 'Sister, since I was born, I do not recall that I have ever intentionally deprived a living being of life. By this truth, may you and your infant be well.'

Venerable sir, wouldn't I be telling a deliberate lie? For I have intentionally deprived living beings of life.
?

Then, Angulimala, say to that woman, 'Sister, since I was born with the noble birth, I do not recall that I have ever intentionally deprived a living being of life. By this truth, may you and your infant be well.'
Yes, venerable sir.
'Noble birth', in this context, can reasonably be taken to indicate his transformation into a bhikku.
अपनी आशाओं से अधिक पाइए
MONEY EXCHANGE
ALLAHA AD
BANK

Joginder, how old are you?
Uh ... seventeen or eighteen. But, like, at school my age is twelve.
How come?
I was told to sit in a lower class.
Do you have siblings?
Two sisters and three brothers. It's like ... everyone is married, I'm the youngest.
Did you convert to Buddhism or are your parents Buddhist?
Parents are Buddhist.
So ... do you know about the Buddha's teachings?
Not really ...

No one tells you?
No, uh, we go to the Buddha temple where they give us a mat to sit on. Then they say something on the mike and we repeat.
Do you know what they say?
They repeat many times but I don't remember.
Do you worship at home?
Yes ... it's like ... we have a nice little temple behind our house. We believe all gods, Buddha, Ram, Shivji ...
And what do your parents do?
Sir, they do farming, and they run a general store.

Was the food okay, sir?
Ya, it was very good!
Are you going to have tomorrow's lunch?
Yes, we will.
TOK
TOK

BADA BADA BADA

TOURIST B

SRAVAS

WHIZZ

Isn't he the same guy we saw on the day we arrived?

...

What do they call it?
The Thais call it Mahamongkol.
Srr
Srr
The stupa is still being made. I'll show you the Buddha statue.
Namaste! You are Indian?
Yes.
Hindu?
No, Buddhist.
Ah! You come for vipassana meditation course?
No, no, we are just travelling.
That's very nice! Please take this. Please leave footwear here.
Thank you!

Strange place!
Ya, strange ... this Buddhist paradise in the middle of rural poverty.
On the other hand, it represents a Buddhist revival of sorts.
In Kushinagar, a group wants to build a gigantic Maitreya Buddha as tall as the Statue of Liberty!
Please wash your feet before entering the meditation hall.

That was so different from a Hindu temple, no?

Hmm ... it seems this organization was started by a Thai beautician-turned-Buddhist nun. Weirdly, this brochure has no contact details of the organization.

I don't know ... something about these personality-driven groups makes me nervous.
Srv
Srv

Ya ... it's as if they live in a fantasy of their own making.
Srv
Srv

Srv
Srv

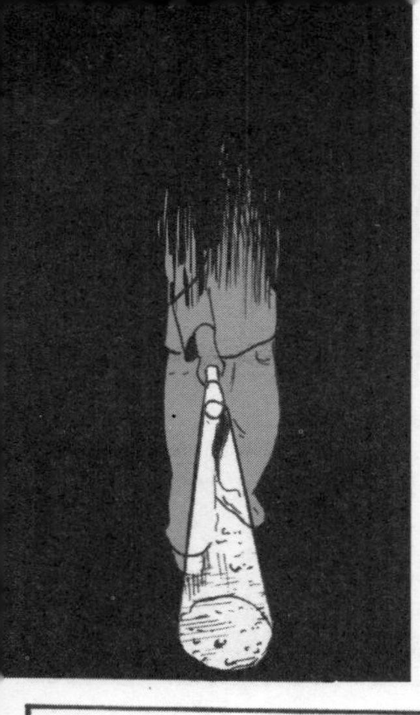

Come, please sit. There's no power, so we are sitting outside in the breeze. Inside is too hot.

It's Haridwar Singh, the hotel manager, and the guy with the bike. Are they drinking?

Please sit, madam. He is in charge of the police station here.

Our police station is right next door!

Joginder, four teas!

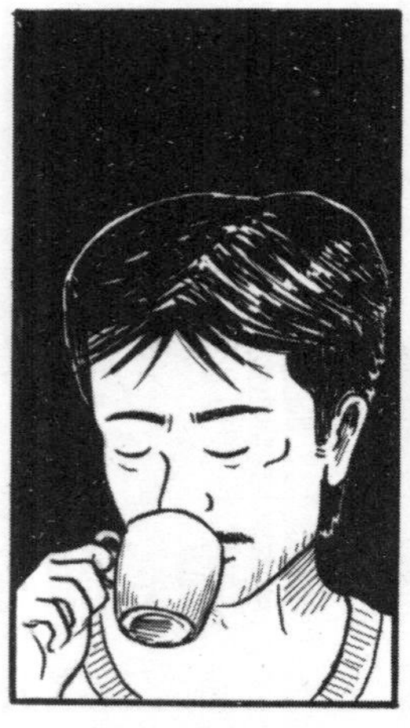

Have you seen *Dabangg*, where Salman Khan is a UP police officer?

Yes. I liked it. It's a hit film!

I also liked it ... I am also a UP police officer, but real life is so different from movies. Sometimes it gets very boring in this village.

Are there Maoists in this area?

No, no! You see Maoists are mostly on the Bihar side. It's okay here, no pressure. Haha!

But then, here too, since the tourists have increased, there have been some incidents ... like about a year ago, a Thai lady was murdered.

There was a boy, about twenty—twenty-five, a nice boy, spoke English well. He was studying for the IAS exam, and he also used to be a guide to tourists.

That's how he met this Thai lady. Impressed, she began giving him some money.

That then developed into a relationship, and she kept coming back. This went on for two years.

One day, about a year ago, this boy told the woman that he would like to show her a new site behind the Angulimala stupa.

At the deserted site, he noticed some money in the purse she had opened.

Filled with greed for money, he hit her right there with a stone. She died on the spot.

There were just 40,000 rupees in the purse.

Think about it, if he had just continued with that relationship, how much more he could have earned!

So how did you get him?

That wasn't difficult. We got the information immediately.

Is he in jail now?

Ah. The light back!

Right now he's in jail, but he's not yet convicted. All that takes time, no?

And he is fighting the panchayat elections, can you imagine?

There are forty candidates this time!

ha ha ha ha!

The MLA is coming here tomorrow, for the election campaign.

Joginder was telling us about it.

Madam, they will do anything for votes, even kidnapping!

Kidnapping?

As in, they pick up some influential people from the villages and make them stay in a hotel or some such place elsewhere.
They give them food and drinks and keep them there until the elections are over, making sure they get their people to vote for them. Isn't that kidnapping?
Hmm ... I think we should leave now. We have a train to catch early tomorrow morning.
Sure. You can go have your dinner now.
Joginder! Is the food ready?
Yes sir!
It was nice meeting you.
Same here.

Isn't that Angulimala, the murderer?
Of course it is! Heard he's become a disciple of that celebrity Sakyan monk, Siddhatta.
WHOOP!
THAD
Now you pay for your actions, Angulimala!

Bear with it, brahman. Bear with it. The fruit of the kamma that would have burnt you in hell for many thousand years, you are experiencing in the here and now.
KHAT
KHAT
KHAT
Haan, Joginder?
The vehicle has arrived.

TRR TATARR...

THAAP

Oh, a dargah!

RELIGION
& FITCH

5.
City and Monastery

You are Hindu, right?
Ya, ya, of course ... uh ... I respect everyone.
No, no. I was just asking.
By caste I am Rajput.
Uff! He thinks we were trying to know his caste ... were we?

LUX
VENUS

नालन्दा टाँगा

GOVT. OF INDIA
ARCHAEOLOG
NALANDA
Darrr

I'm Choudhury. We spoke on the phone.
COLD WATER
You see, there's going to be an election in Bihar now, so some MLAs could visit. If they come, you will have to shift.
Are you sure they're going to come?
It's generally empty. They come only during elections. But I'm not sure.
Bihari culture is so different from UP. More affinity to Bengal than to the north, I think.
Ya! As a Bihari, I should know.

A mango tree!
The Pali suttas speak of a mango grove at Nalanda where the Tathagata discoursed.
Bharath, why don't you go have a bath?

This is not the real gate of Nalanda.
It was made by breaking the wall.
The original gate has not yet been traced.
This was a three-storey building, and each student had a single room.
Please come this way.

Many of these monastic buildings use bricks shaped like slabs rather than the blocks we use today.

ancient brick slab

modern brick block

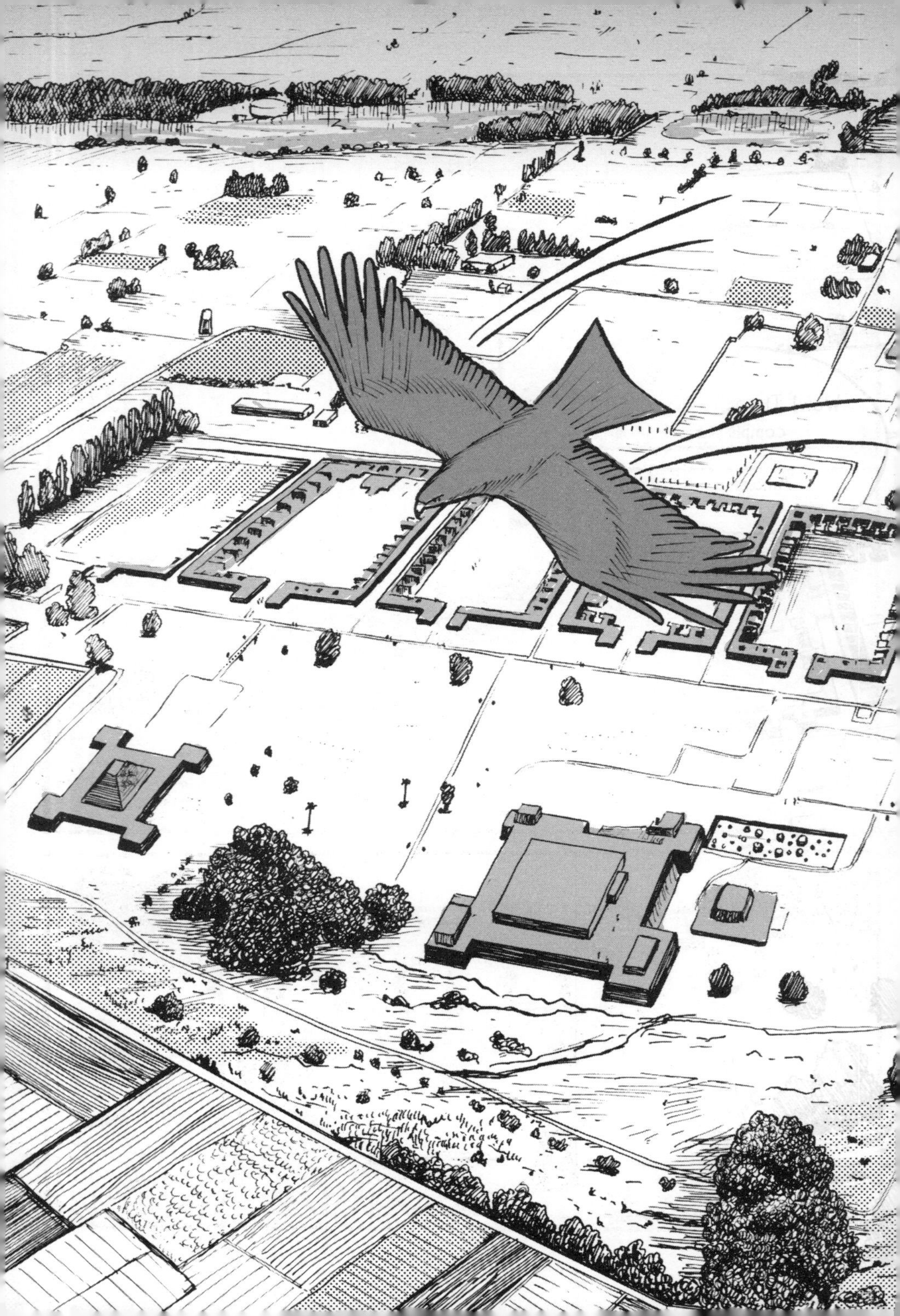

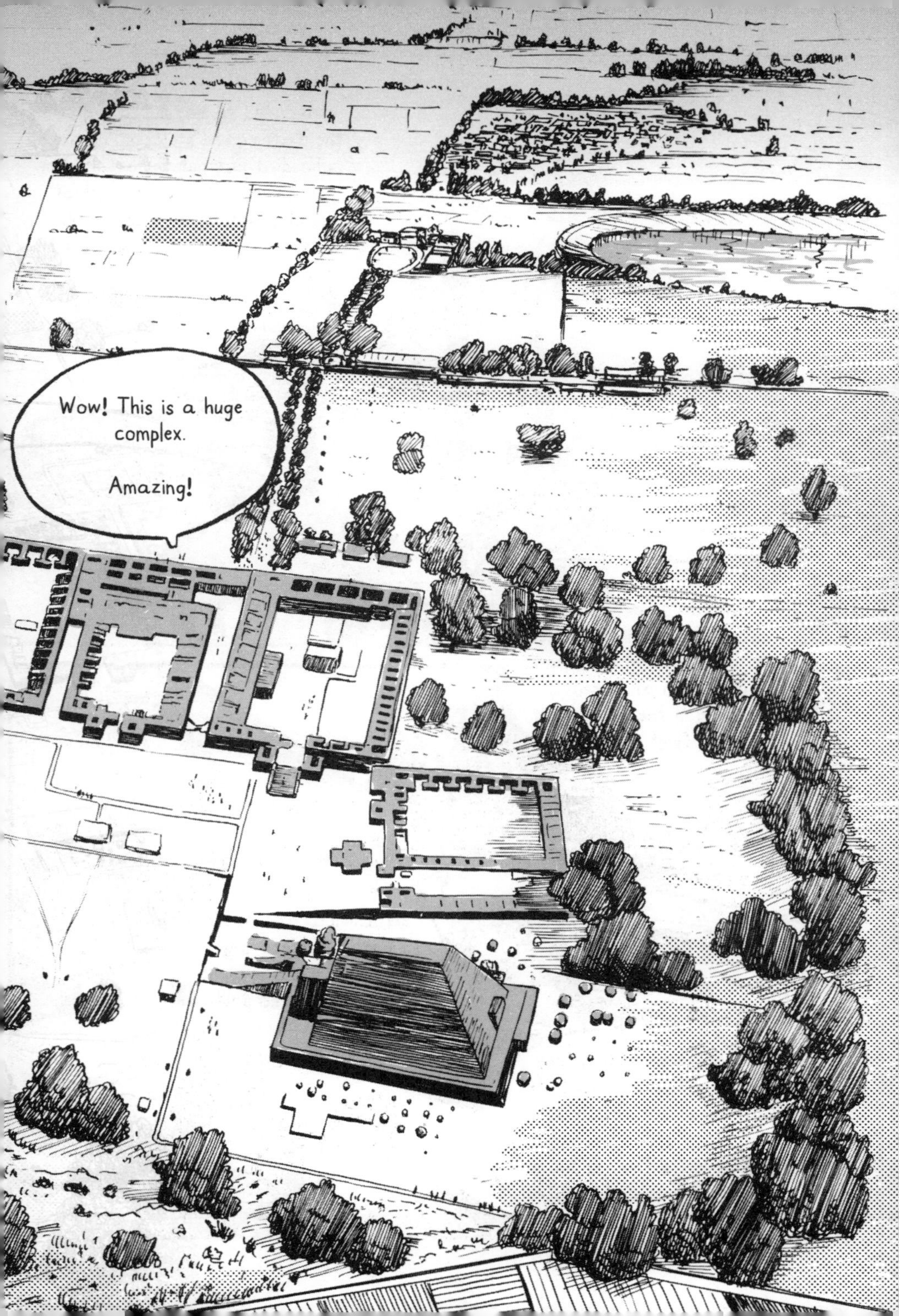
Wow! This is a huge complex.
Amazing!

The iconic stupa at Nalanda is dedicated to Sariputta, one of the Tathagata's closest disciples, who died just months before him and lived in Nalanda most of his life. Ashoka built the earliest stupa here, but it doesn't exist anymore. The current structure dates from the fifth century CE, during the Gupta era.
Nalanda's fame as a centre of learning coincides with the period when Puranic Vaishnavism and Shaivism developed in the latter half of the first millennium.
Ya. It seems both brahminical and Buddhist thought developed together, even though they are philosophically and politically opposed to each other.
As rival faiths, they appear equally poised. Yet, by the end of the thirteenth century, Buddhism practically disappears from India and not a single Buddhist text survives here.
Hmm ... bizarre!

Oh!
A dead end.

Tibetan monks completely fit into this picture, no?

That reminds me of something the Dalai Lama reiterates ...

The Tibetan Buddhist tradition is essentially the Nalanda tradition.

Ironically, it is because the Buddhists of Tibet fled the Chinese occupation that the Nalanda tradition is back in India.
Just as Indian Buddhist monks had fled to Tibet after the Islamic conquest 800 years ago.
The movement was most probably gradual, as is true of the Tibetan migration too. Refugees from Tibet keep coming in even today.
Hmm ... I suppose Buddhist society and culture crucially depend on the Sangha.
If support to the Sangha is cut off, Buddhism is finished in that region. The Chinese had in fact adopted Buddhism in the second century CE, much before the Tibetans themselves.

Xuanzang, the best known of Chinese Buddhist travellers, stayed here for two years, during 637–39 CE, translating Sanskrit Buddhist texts.

Xuanzang, 11th c. painting from Dunhuang caves, China.

When did you say Xuanzang came to India?
That must be 630–45 CE. Fifteen years for the whole trip.
Nalanda was burnt in 1198 after a raid led by Bakhtiyar Khilji, a Turkic general under Qutubuddin Aibak, the first sultan of Delhi.
The Prophet Mohammed died in 632 CE. Xuanzang lived during the beginning of Islam.
Oh ya! That's a strange coincidence.

Nalanda was only gradually abandoned. In 1235, Chag Lotsawa, a Tibetan monk, visited and left an account. Turkish and Afghan soldiers had encamped at the nearby Odantapuri monastery. There were some seventy monks-in-residence in spite of a recent attack. Another Tibetan text, the *Pag Sam Jon Zang*, claims that repairs were carried out by Muditabhadra, a monk. But then, a brahminical temple was erected there at the behest of a Magadhan minister and a fire sacrifice organized. The embers were used to burn Ratnodadhi, one of the remaining libraries at Nalanda.

Muslim historian Minhaj referred to the site as 'Bihar' — derived from 'vihara' (monastery) — which is the current name of the region.

This palm tree is very special! Usually it has only a single trunk but this one has eight branches, just like Buddhism, which is the Eightfold Path! HAHA!
...

Chir
Chir
chir
Chir
Chir
chir
chir
Chir
Chir
Chir
chir
Chir
Chir
chir
chir
Chir

Chir
Chir

GUTURR

GOVT. OF INDIA

KHAT
KHAT

It's me, Choudhury. Hope I am not disturbing you?

Uh ... have you had your dinner?
Yes.
I have brought you some home-made curd, please have.
That's a lot of curd, and full of cream. I can't have it!

So ... have you seen everything in Nalanda?
Yes. Tomorrow we will go to Rajgir.
Has there been more digging here recently?

Not recently. The area is surrounded by villages and farmland. They won't vacate the land. Most of the ASI money is spent on maintenance ... but you see, the recent Ayodhya verdict was based on the ASI report!

We conducted an excavation at Ayodhya in 2003, and that proved the existence of the temple.

...

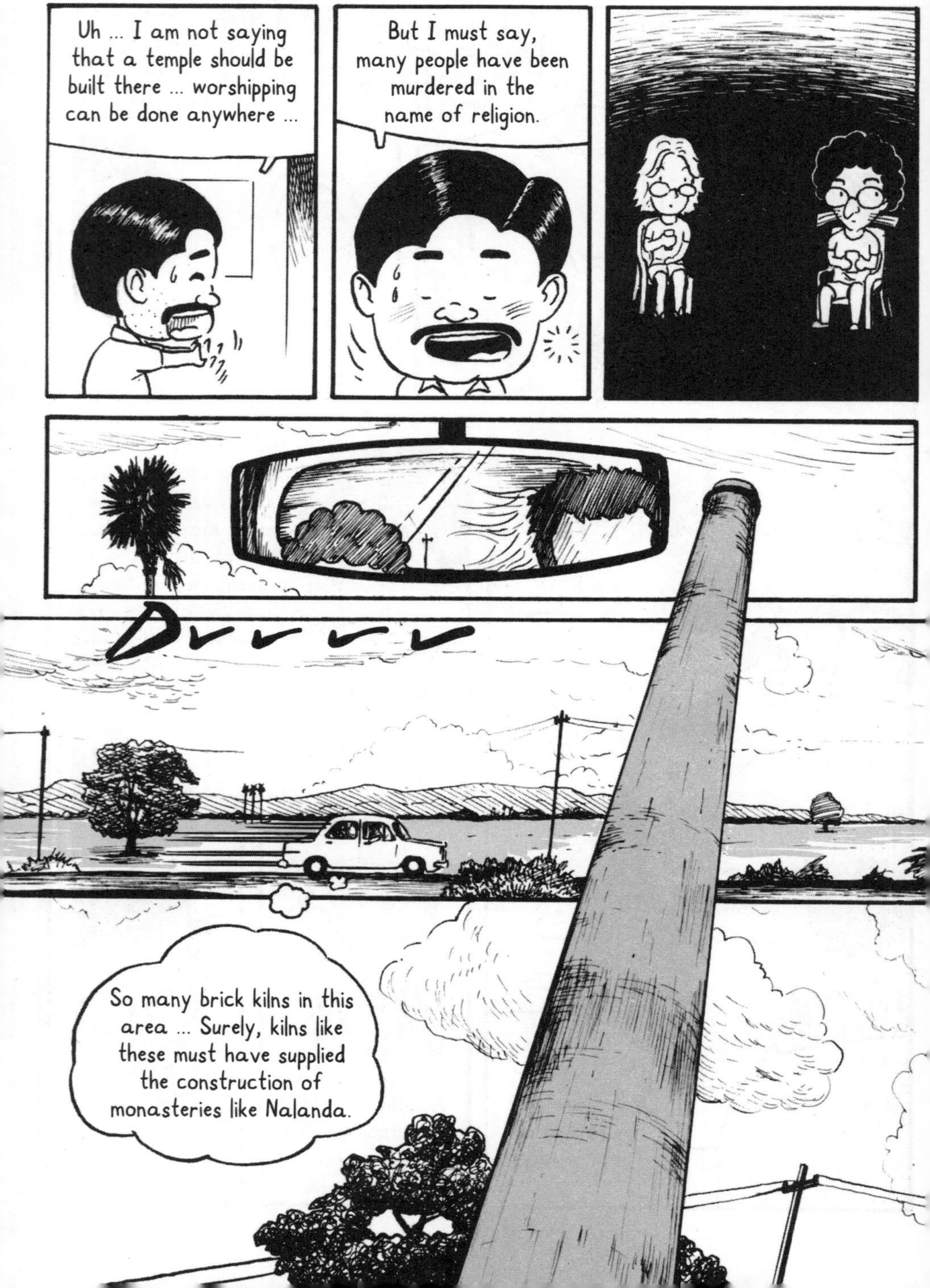

Uh ... I am not saying that a temple should be built there ... worshipping can be done anywhere ...

But I must say, many people have been murdered in the name of religion.

Drrrrr
So many brick kilns in this area ... Surely, kilns like these must have supplied the construction of monasteries like Nalanda.

These hills are just like how Osamu Tezuka drew them in his comics.
Dvvvv

Where do you want to go first?
There's the Sonbhandar cave ahead.
Hello! I am a certified guide. Which country are you from?
The board outside says it is a Jain cave, but it served both Buddhist and Jain monks. Come, I will show.

See the Buddhist dharmachakra carved here.

This standing figure on the right is Mahavira of the Jain tradition.

Behind this was the vault where King Bimbisara stored the Magadha kingdom's wealth. It is sealed now. The British wanted to break it open but the great Indian scientist A.J.C Bose told them not to.

Nearby is a ruin which is apparently evidence of a gym belonging to Jarasandha, a character from the Mahabharata.
But this mythical reference is already there in the *Buddhacharita*, the monk Ashvaghosha's second-century Sanskrit verse biography of the Buddha.
Myth and history, so deeply interwoven.

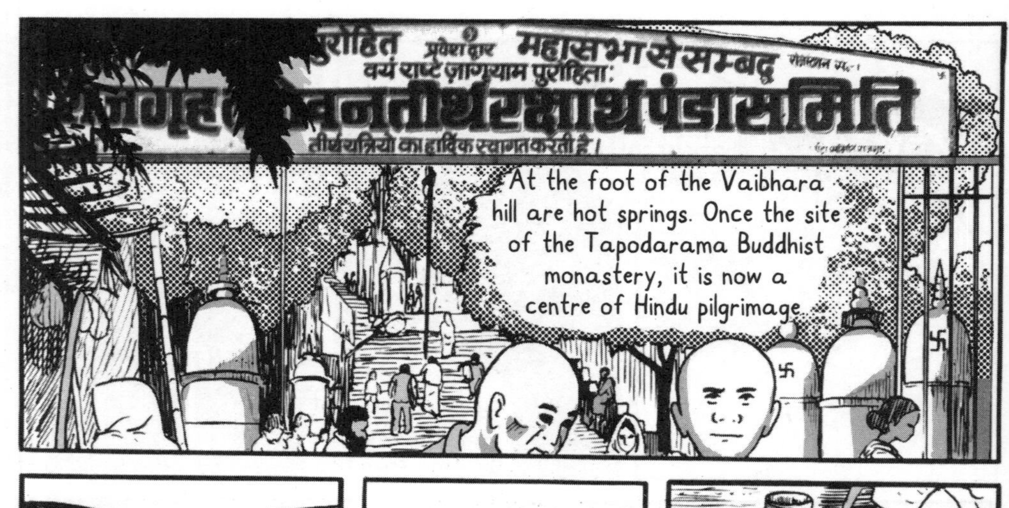
पुरोहित
प्रवेश द्वार
महासभा से सम्बद्ध
वयं राष्ट्रे जागृयाम पुरोहिताः
तीर्थयात्रियों का हार्दिक स्वागत करती है।
At the foot of the Vaibhara hill are hot springs. Once the site of the Tapodarama Buddhist monastery, it is now a centre of Hindu pilgrimage.

It's hot!

Hello!

Which country you are? Temple here ... down ...

(Hindi) We want to go up to see the cave.

Oh, you are Hindu ... okay. Where are you from? Husband wife?

Yes, husband wife ... We are from Delhi.

Okay, please take this prasad.

No, thank you.
You have come from far away, please don't refuse! It is god's blessing.

Uh ... we are Buddhists ... we've come to see the cave.

Okay, so say 'Buddham sharanam gachchhami'. Now take the prasad.
?!

Why are you forcing us?

...

The priest at the Jain temple behind us was asking for 'bakhsheesh'.
Fyuu!
Tired
Oh! Did you give?
No.

Ah! There it is, the Sattapanni cave.

In the Pali suttas, most of the discourses begin with 'Evam me sutam' — Thus I have heard — thereby affirming that these words are the testimony of a human narrator and not the revelation of a god. According to the suttas, the first Buddhist Council was convened by the elder monk Mahakassapa under the aegis of King Ajatasattu soon after the Tathagata's death. The suttas and the Vinaya were recited and memorized. The event was held around a cave in one of the hills surrounding Rajgriha. However, no archaeological evidence exists, so the current location is only symbolic.

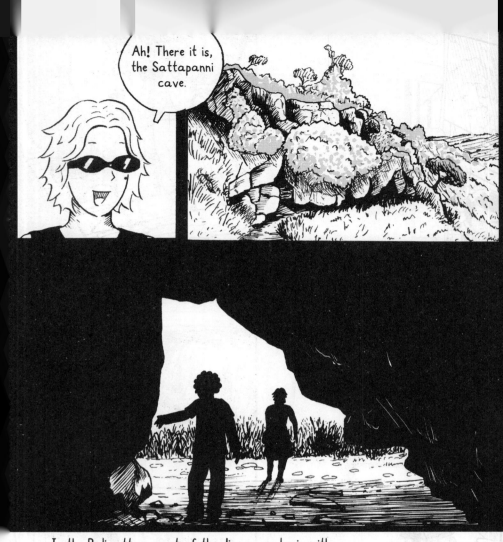

ICKET
/- PER HEAD
WAY TO CHAIRLIFT
रोपवे चढने का रास्ता
BIHAR STATE TOURISM
PLEASE KEEP PREMISE

91

बिहार
पर्यटन
93

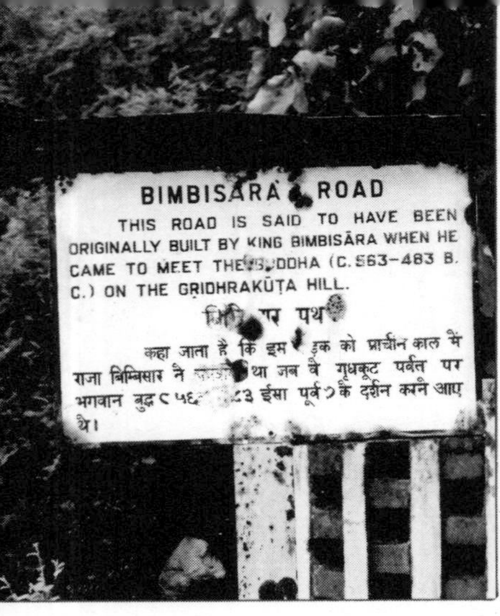
BIMBISARA ROAD
THIS ROAD IS SAID TO HAVE BEEN ORIGINALLY BUILT BY KING BIMBISĀRA WHEN HE CAME TO MEET THE BUDDHA (C. 563-483 B. C.) ON THE GRIDHRAKŪṬA HILL.

That ropeway was shaky. Even stopped midway a few times!
Ya, scary!

AHH! Langurs!

Go, go, they won't harm.

The rocks
actually resemble
vultures!

Vulture's Peak is mentioned several times
in the Pali suttas as the spot where the
Tathagata lived and taught at Rajgriha.

Evam me sutam ...

I have heard that ...

... on one occasion the Blessed One was staying near Rajgriha on Vulture's Peak mountain, in the bear's cave. Then ...

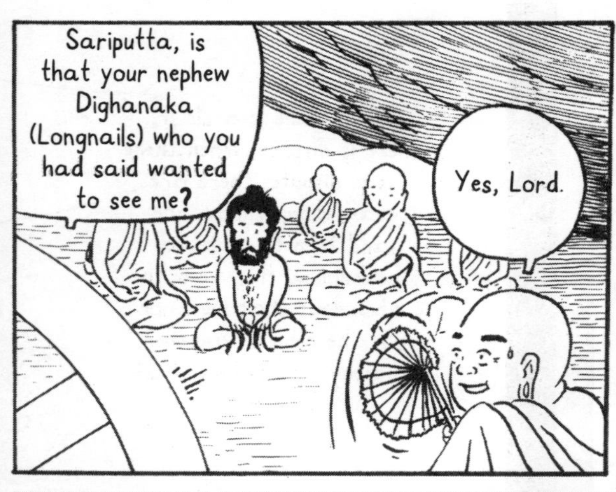

Sariputta, is that your nephew Dighanaka (Longnails) who you had said wanted to see me?
Yes, Lord.

Master Gotama, I am of the view that 'all is not pleasing to me'.

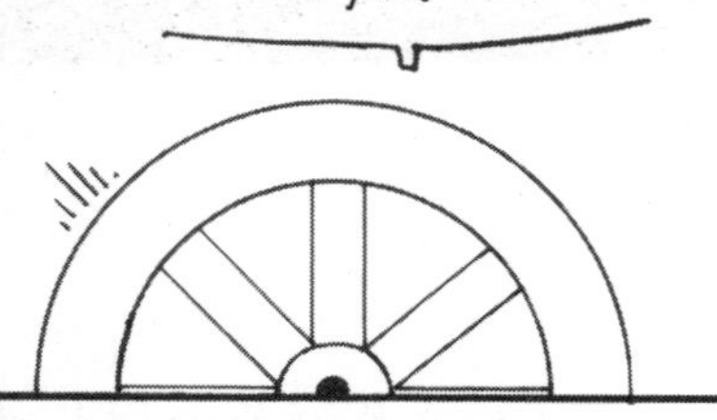

But even this view of yours, 'all is not pleasing to me' — is even that not pleasing to you?

Even if this view of mine were pleasing to me, Master Gotama, it would still be the same, still be the same.

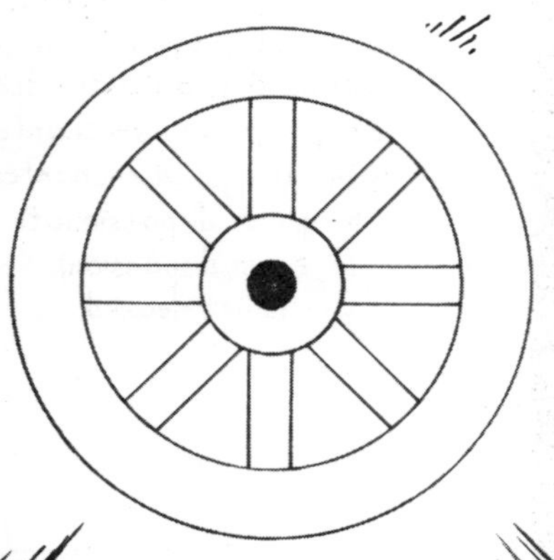

Well, Dighanaka, there are more than many in the world who say 'It would still be same', yet they do not abandon that view and cling to another view instead. There are even fewer who abandon that view and do not then cling to another.

A wise person who holds views considers this: if I were to firmly hold on to this view of mine and insist that only this is true and all else is worthless, I would clash with other views and opinions.

When there is a clash, there is dispute. When there is a dispute, there are quarrelling, annoyance, and then frustration. Envisioning this, he both abandons that view nor does he cling to another, thereby relinquishing these views.

Now, Dighanaka, this body, endowed with form, born of mother and father, is subject to inconsistency, to pain, dissolution, dispersion, disintegration, emptiness, not-self. Thus envisioning it, any desire for the body is abandoned.

There are these three kinds of feeling: pleasant, painful and neither-pleasant-nor-painful. These feelings are inconsistent, fabricated, dependently co-arisen, subject to ending. Seeing this, an instructed disciple grows disenchanted with feelings. Disenchanted, he grows dispassionate. From dispassion, he is released.

With release, there is the knowledge 'released'. He discerns, birth is ended, the holy life fulfilled, the task done. There is nothing further for this world.

A monk whose mind is thus released does not take sides with anyone, does not dispute with anyone. He words things by means of what is said in the world but without grasping at it.

Indeed, it seems that the Blessed One speaks to us of abandoning each of these mental qualities through direct knowledge.

Whatever is subject to origination is all subject to cessation.

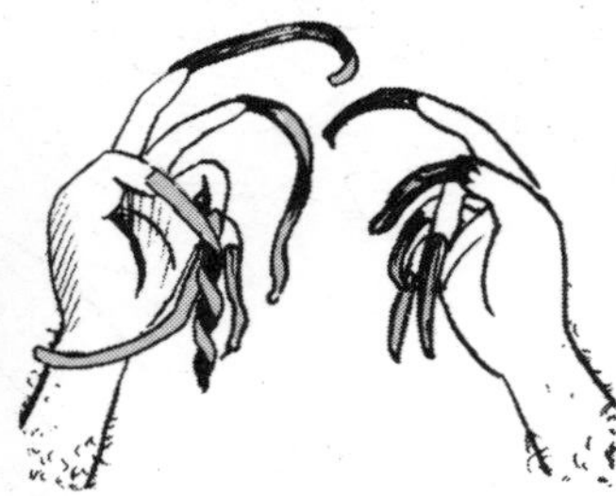

Magnificent Master Gotama! Just as if one were to carry a lamp into the dark, so has Master Gotama, through many lines of reasoning, made the Dhamma clear.

I go to Master Gotama for refuge, to the Dhamma, to the Sangha. May he remember me as a lay follower who has gone to him for refuge from this day onward, for life.

6.
Path Regained

Prince Bodhi, before my Awakening, I too had the idea that happiness could not be reached through happiness, but only through pain.

Plut!

SPLASH
So after some time, while still a young man, against the wishes of my parents, I shaved off my hair and beard, put on ochre robes, and went forth into homelessness, in quest of the ultimate state of peace.
I approached Alara Kalama, and later Uddaka Ramaputta, both of whose teachings I mastered, but it occurred to me that they did not help bring about direct knowledge, nor Awakening.

I continued my journey through Magadha until I reached the army township of Uruvela, a delightful place with a river and villages nearby for seeking alms.

So, Prince Bodhi, I decided that I might grit my teeth and mentally hold down my mind, crush it, overwhelm it and, yet, while the mindfulness I established was free of confusion, I was exhausted by this effort.

I practised cutting out food entirely, so that some gods who saw me thought that I was dead. And then it occurred to me that ascetics in the past had not experienced pain beyond this extreme, nor will present or future ascetics. I had achieved no special knowledge and insight as a result of this. Might there be in fact another path to Awakening?

Fasting Buddha, 2nd–3rd c. CE, Gandhara. Lahore Museum.

Then I remembered that once, when I was sitting in the cool shade of a roseapple tree while my Sakyan father was engaged in work, I had attained the joy and happiness of the first *jhana, which is accompanied by thinking and examining, and is born of seclusion.

Might this, in fact, not be the path to Awakening? I asked myself why I feared this happiness, which had nothing to do with sense pleasures and unwholesome qualities.

*Jhana (dhyana). Meditative absorption, in four stages, according to Buddhist teaching.

It would not be easy to achieve this happiness with a body that had become emaciated, so I thought I should take some solid food, some rice gruel.

After I had taken the food, the five monks who were with me thought, 'The ascetic Gotama is one for excess! He has given up the struggle.'

They lost their enthusiasm for me and left.

Once I had taken solid food and regained my strength,
I lived completely secluded from sense desires and unwholesome qualities of mind,
having attained the equanimity of the fourth jhana.

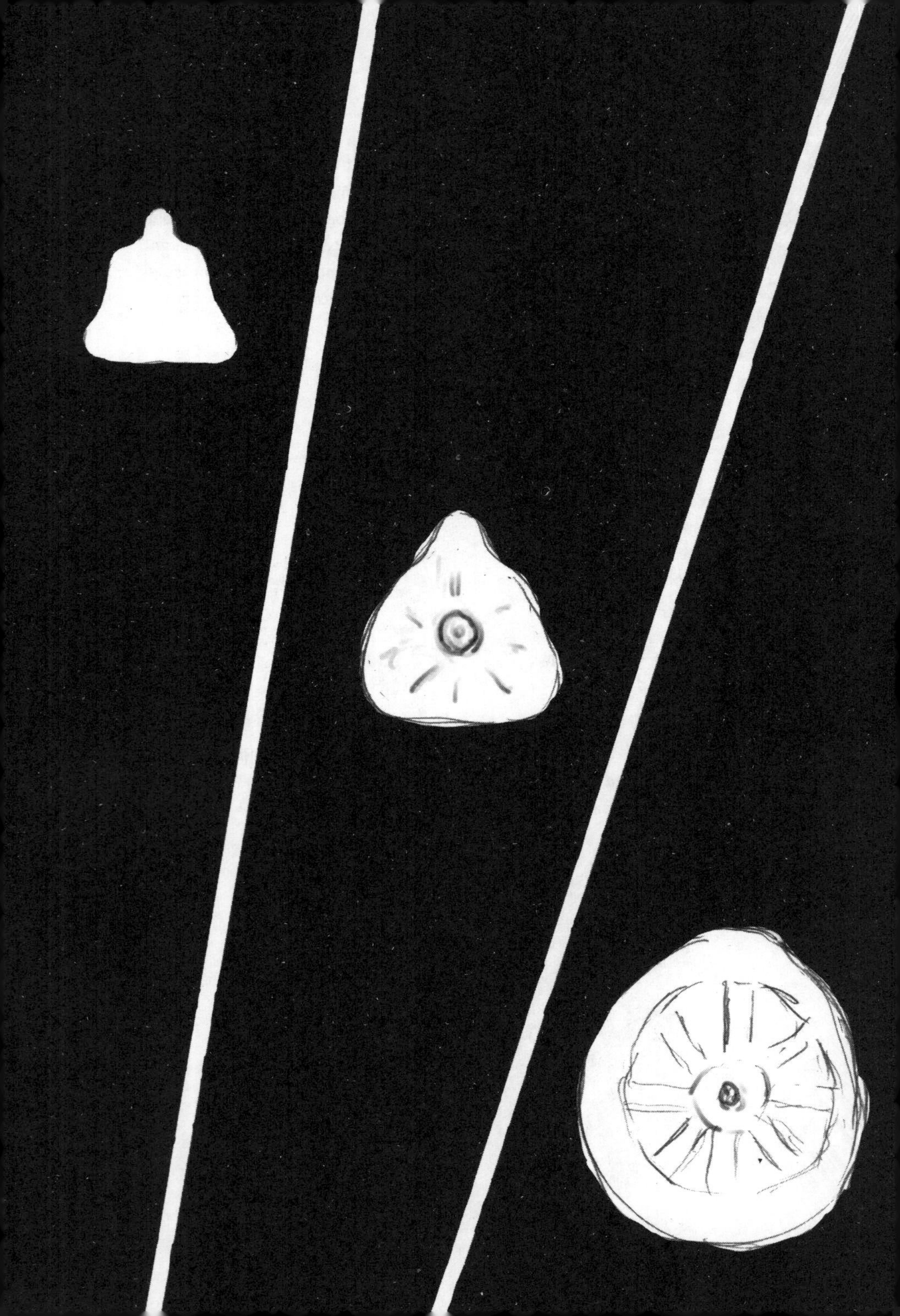

This moment, the result of Siddhatta Gotama's
six-year effort, came to be
referred to as Nirvana
(extinguishing of the causes of suffering).

He was thirty-five years old.

The site of this human achievement was
venerated by the followers of his teaching even
during his own lifetime, and has since become
the most sacred place for Buddhists,
known today as Bodhgaya.

Relief sculpture at Sanchi stupa, 2nd c. BCE.

Ashoka built the first temple next to the Bodhi tree, and installed the Diamond Throne (Vajrasana). It is said that his devotion to the tree was such that he once fainted at the sight of it. The current temple dates from the fifth century CE, and is the oldest standing brick temple structure in India.

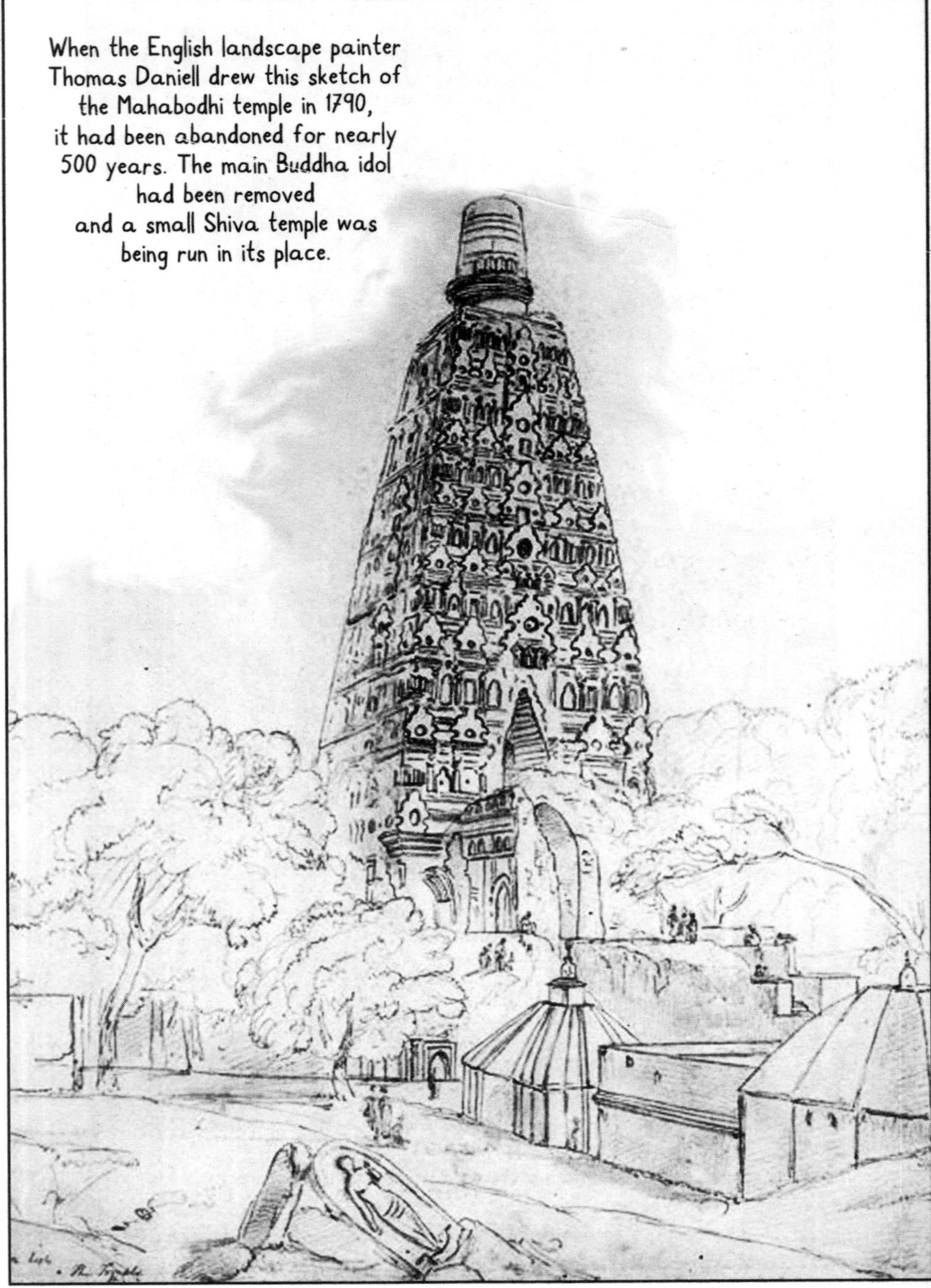
When the English landscape painter
Thomas Daniell drew this sketch of
the Mahabodhi temple in 1790,
it had been abandoned for nearly
500 years. The main Buddha idol
had been removed
and a small Shiva temple was
being run in its place.

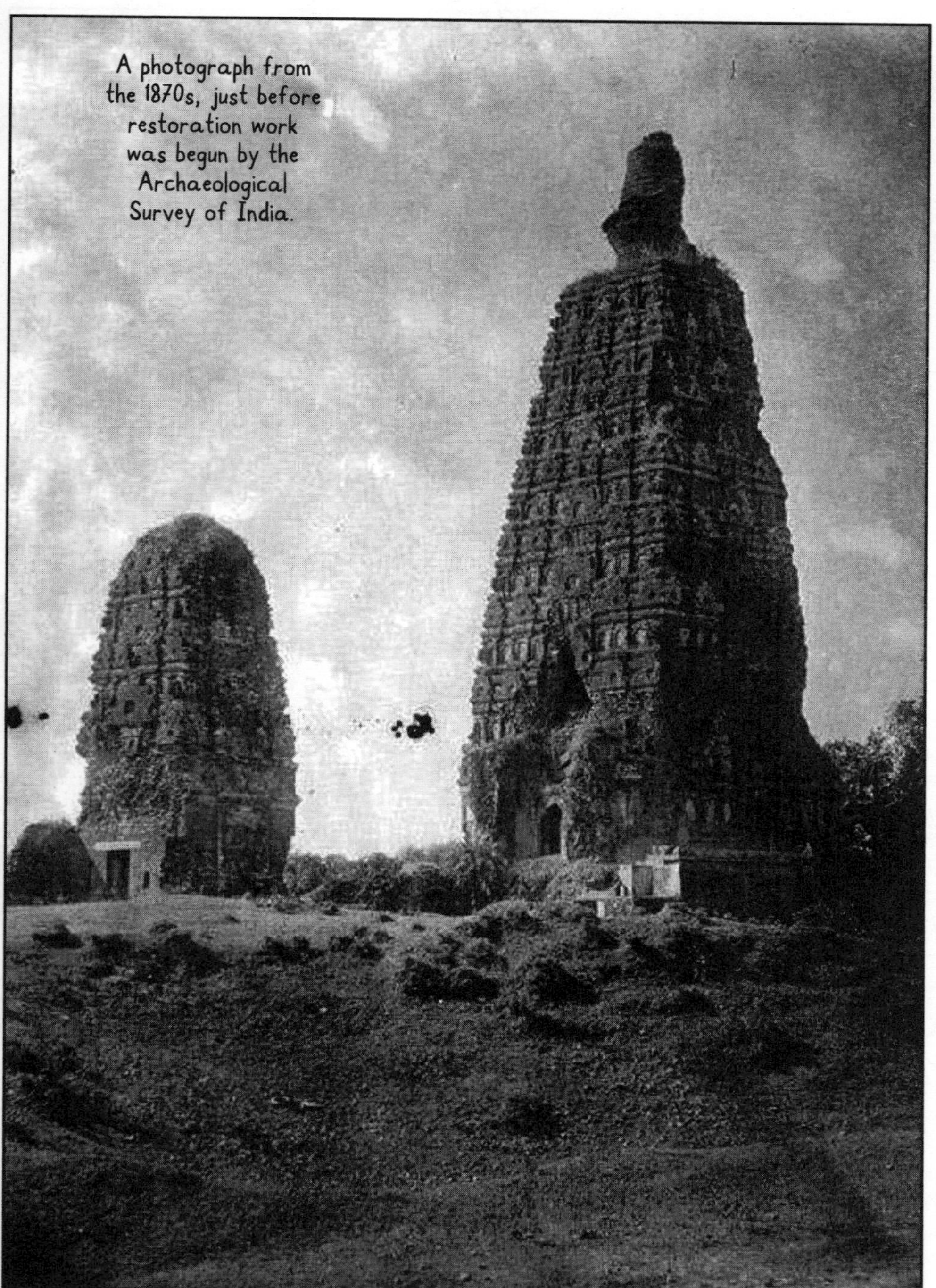

A photograph from the 1870s, just before restoration work was begun by the Archaeological Survey of India.

AJAPALA NIGRODHA TREE (BANYAN TREE)
LORD BUDDHA SPENT THE FIFTH WEEK UNDER THIS TREE IN MEDITATION AFTER ENLIGHTENMENT. HERE HE REPLIED TO A BRAHMANA THAT ONLY BY ONE'S DEEDS ONE BECOMES A BRAHMANA, NOT BY BIRTH.
A retort to brahminism and casteism right at the entrance!

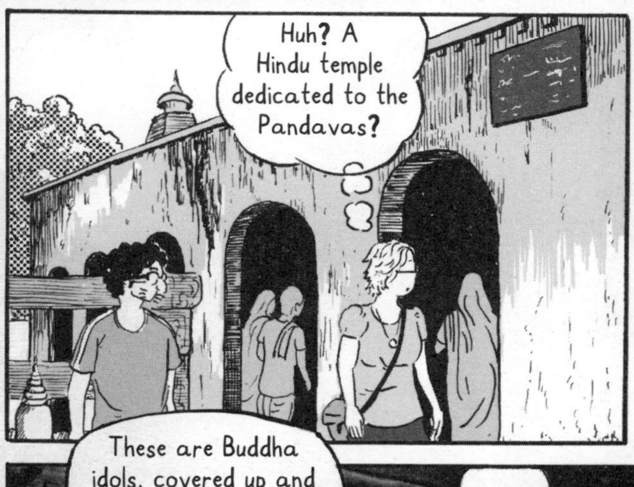
Huh? A Hindu temple dedicated to the Pandavas?

Sanatan Dharma
Pancho Pandov
Mahadeo Giri
Chetan Giri
Visit
सनातन धर्म
पाँच पाण्डव
महादेव गिरि
दर्शन
आदेशानुसार
बोधगया मठ

These are Buddha idols, covered up and passed off as images of the Pandavas!
Weird! Wonder what Buddhist pilgrims think of this.
I suppose they just ignore it. Let's see the main temple.

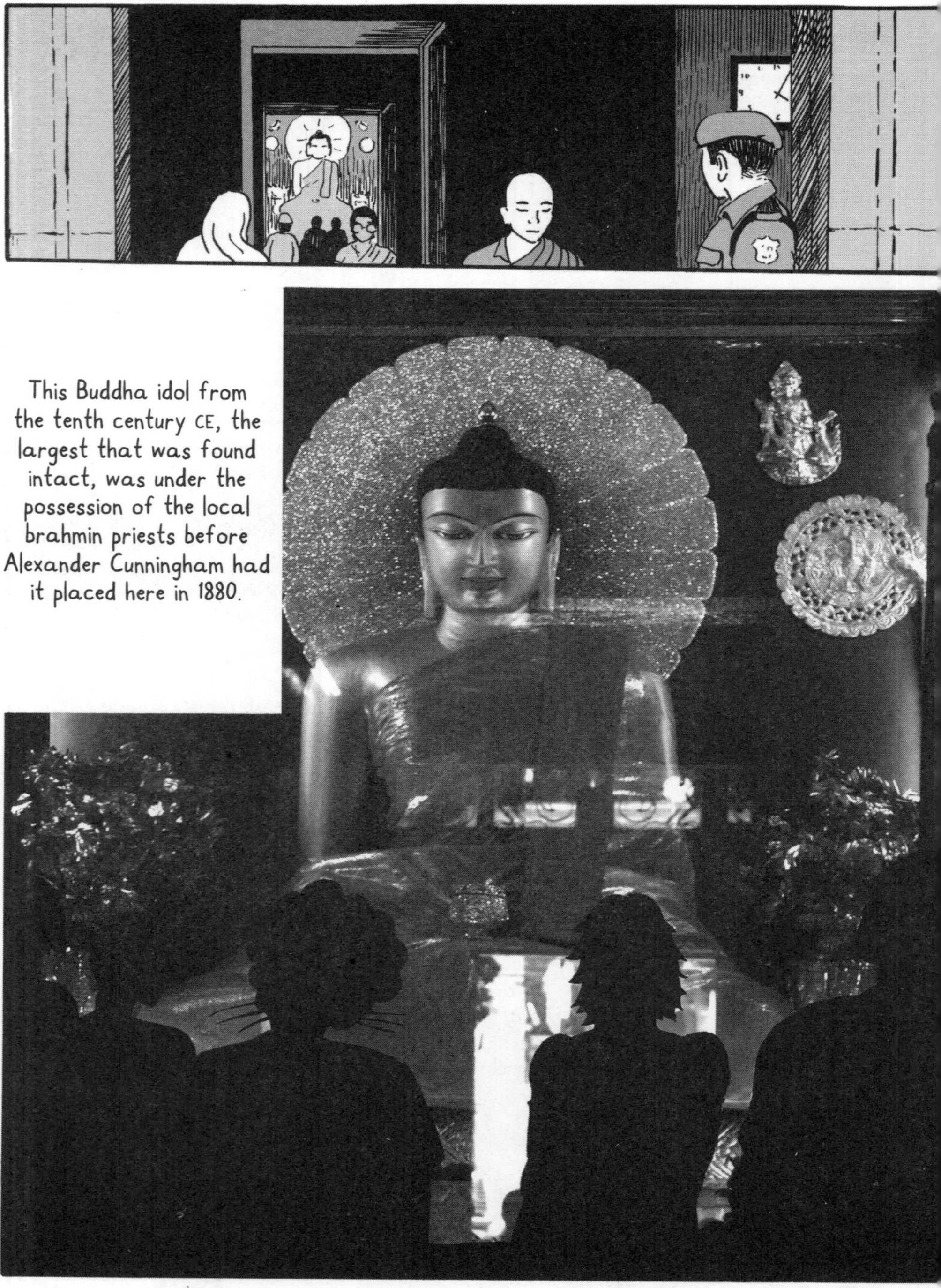

This Buddha idol from the tenth century CE, the largest that was found intact, was under the possession of the local brahmin priests before Alexander Cunningham had it placed here in 1880.

Ah! The Bodhi tree is behind the temple.

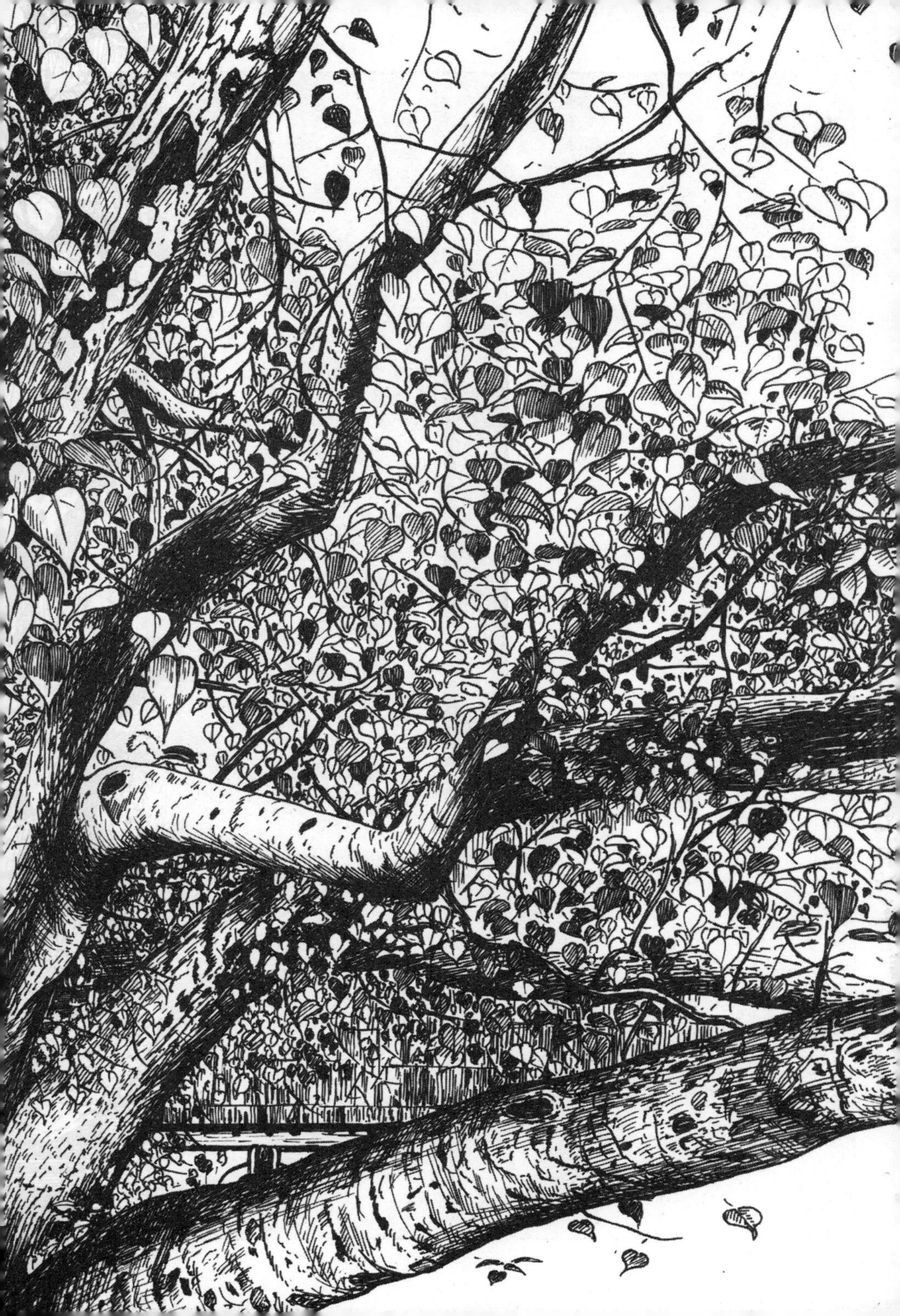

The end of the world can never be reached
Through travelling,
Yet, without reaching the end,
There is no release from suffering.

Therefore, the wise one, knowing the world,
Goes to the end, having fulfilled the holy life.
Knowing the world's end, he is still,
Not wishing for this world nor another.

From the Samyutta Nikaya, Sutta Pitaka, first century BCE.

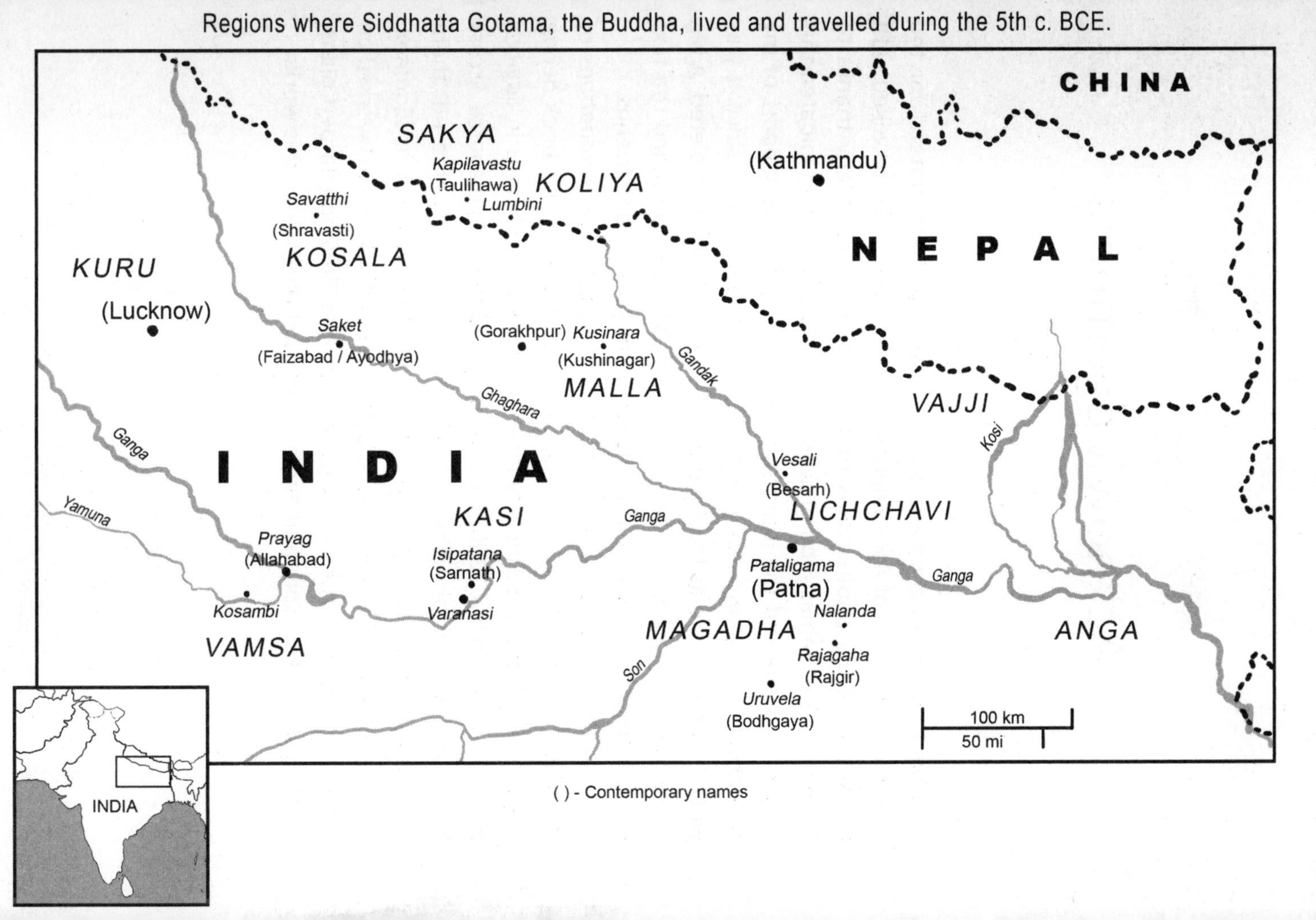
Regions where Siddhatta Gotama, the Buddha, lived and travelled during the 5th c. BCE.
CHINA
SAKYA
Kapilavastu
(Taulihawa)
KOLIYA
Lumbini
(Kathmandu)
Savatthi
(Shravasti)
KOSALA
NEPAL
KURU
(Lucknow)
Saket
(Faizabad / Ayodhya)
(Gorakhpur)
Kusinara
(Kushinagar)
Gandak
MALLA
Ghaghara
VAJJI
Kosi
Ganga
INDIA
Vesali
(Besarh)
Yamuna
KASI
Ganga
LICHCHAVI
Prayag
(Allahabad)
Isipatana
(Sarnath)
Pataligama
(Patna)
Ganga
Kosambi
Varanasi
Nalanda
MAGADHA
ANGA
VAMSA
Rajagaha
(Rajgir)
Son
Uruvela
(Bodhgaya)
100 km
50 mi
INDIA
( ) - Contemporary names

Acknowledgements

This book has been a long time in the making. I am grateful for the continuous support of Alka Singh, wife and partner, who travelled with me and took the photographs that are in this book. Many thanks to Krishnamurthy Ramasubbu of *Dinamalar* newspaper, who initiated this project and enabled the journey. I am thankful for the support of my colleagues at Film and Television Institute of India, Pune, since it was while I worked there as faculty that half the book was completed. A big thank you to Ajitha G.S., editor at HarperCollins, who refined the text and images. Finally, a debt of gratitude to my parents and friends.

For historical facts, I relied on Rupert Gethin's *The Foundations of Buddhism* (Oxford, 1998). The Pali suttas illustrated in this book derive largely from Rupert Gethin's wonderful English translations in *Sayings of the Buddha* (Oxford, 2008). I also consulted the web resource *Access To Insight (*accesstoinsight.org). I have, however, rephrased them occasionally. Richard Gombrich's *What the Buddha Thought* (Equinox, 2009) greatly enriched my understanding of Buddhism while I worked on the book. Osamu Tezuka's manga masterpiece *Buddha* (HarperCollins, 2006) was a huge inspiration and a formative influence on this work.

About the author

Bharath Murthy is a film-maker and comics author. He studied painting at the Faculty of Fine Arts, M.S. University of Baroda, and film direction at Satyajit Ray Film and Television Institute, Kolkata. His film work includes a feature documentary *The Fragile Heart of Moé* (2010), about comics subcultures in Tokyo, co-produced with NHK (Japan Broadcasting Corporation). Since 2012, he has taught film direction at FTII (Film and Television Institute of India) Pune. *The Vanished Path* is his first book-length comic.

He blogs at http://bcomix.wordpress.com and can be reached at actionist@gmail.com.